Adolescents
on the Edge

Adolescents
on the Edge

Stories and Lessons to Transform Learning

Jimmy Santiago Baca
ReLeah Cossett Lent

HEINEMANN
Portsmouth, NH

Heinemann
361 Hanover Street
Portsmouth, NH 03801–3912
www.heinemann.com

Offices and agents throughout the world

Acknowledgments for borrowed material can be found on page xvi.

Library of Congress Cataloging-in-Publication Data
Baca, Jimmy Santiago.
    Adolescents on the edge : stories and lessons to transform learning / Jimmy Santiago Baca, ReLeah Cossett Lent.
        p. cm.
    Includes bibliographical references.
    ISBN-10: 0-325-02691-2
    ISBN-13: 978-0-325-02691-6
    1. Special education—United States. 2. Children with disabilities—Education—United States. 3. Children with social disabilities—Education—United States. 4. Learning disabled children—Education—United States.   I. Lent, ReLeah Cossett.   II. Title.
LC4015.B25 2010
371.9'0473—dc22   2010000957

Editor: Lisa Luedeke
Production: Vicki Kasabian
DVD producer/director: Kevin Carlson
DVD postproduction services: Pip Clews, Pip Productions
Cover design: Lisa A. Fowler
Cover photography: Steven St. John Photography
Author photograph of Jimmy Santiago Baca: Norman Mauskopf
Typesetter: Publishers' Design and Production Services, Inc.
Manufacturing: Valerie Cooper

Printed in the United States of America on acid-free paper
14 13 12 11 10   VP   1 2 3 4 5

Contents

DVD Contents

Acknowledgments

This project would never have been possible without the wisdom, insight, and creative energy of our editor, Lisa Luedeke. From the very beginning, Lisa's editorial direction transformed our ideas into a cohesive whole as she partnered with us in this wonderful endeavor. We are also grateful to the professional video team who made our sessions with students come to life, especially Kevin Carlson, who headed up the project. We want to thank the stars of the DVD, the students at South Valley Academy in Albuquerque, New Mexico, as well as the staff for opening up their classrooms to us as we filmed. We are also deeply appreciative of the professionals at Heinemann, specifically Vicki Kasabian, our production editor, and Lisa Fowler, who designed the covers. Their talents are evident in this book.

The three teachers who appear on the DVD, Sean Ottner, Chris Oglesby, and Herb Lowrie, are symbolic of the many committed and caring educators who work with adolescents each day. We thank them all for making a real difference in the lives of teens.

Jimmy would like to thank his children, Tones, Gabe, Esai, Morgan, and Lucia, and his inspirational muse and partner Stacy. He also acknowledges his friends Arnold Valario, Ruth Dillingham, Jeff Diamond, and Elena Gonzales.

ReLeah's family, as always, contributed to her work in so many ways. She is especially grateful for the sharp eyes, cogent comments, and maddening attention to detail that her husband, Bert, and her father, Don Cossett, provided. The care and time they devoted to this project added immeasurably to the quality of the final text.

Introduction

It was an unseasonably mild winter day in Milwaukee, the roadside snow melting into rivulets under the bright sun, when students arrived on buses at a downtown studio for a writing workshop with Jimmy Santiago Baca. I had seen Jimmy in action and I knew he would mesmerize his audience, his personality melding with the sharp, heart-wrenching stories he would tell.

I watched a particular young man as he loudly entered the room—baseball cap perched on his head, hoodie up high around his neck, pants sagging. He swaggered rather than walked, eyeing Jimmy as if issuing a challenge. As the students settled into a large circle, Jimmy began, the rhythm of his storytelling punctuated with laughter, his voice gaining momentum, booming a line from his narrative, "Man, what did I tell you? You don't mess with family!" or softly repeating his brother's advice when they first arrived at the orphanage, "Quit crying—if you don't, the kids are going to beat you."

While most of the students listened, sizing Jimmy up quietly, the young man I had noticed earlier began smirking, saying something under his breath, elbowing the person sitting beside him in the circle. The challenge gradually became louder, until, finally, his teacher got up from her seat and walked over to the boy. Jimmy said, "No, it's all right," but she knelt beside the boy anyway, whispering softly. As she walked away, his smirk returned, a bit more subdued but still obvious. I couldn't take my eyes off him. Here was the proverbial adolescent on the edge, a young male already in trouble, mocking the very system trying to help him. I waited to see how Jimmy would deal with him, expecting the situation to escalate as it so often does in a classroom but, instead, the tension seemed to diffuse, as if the boy came to realize that he had nothing to push against. He had refused to make eye contact with Jimmy at first, looking away arrogantly, but as the plot of the story began to take shape, I saw him glance sideways at Jimmy.

Then, toward the end, it happened. The shell that this kid lived in, the same one that encases so many students who enter our classes each day, cracked—not a total falling away, but a tiny piercing. It was enough, though. He smiled at something Jimmy said as the others laughed out loud. The smile escaped before he caught himself and returned to his secure, defensive posture.

By the end of the workshop, he had put pen to paper, but making sure we all knew his purpose: "I'm just gonna write something I wanna tell my boys." But, amazingly, he was even coaxed into sharing his writing with the rest of the group at the end of the session. It was only a few lines, perhaps something he had heard elsewhere and claimed as his own, but it didn't matter. He had entered the world of literacy and found satisfaction in the effort.

Jimmy's approach confirmed my own belief, developed during my many years in the classroom, that engagement, relevance, and intrinsic purpose are essential to deep learning. While a high school teacher, I would lie awake at night creating scenarios of ways that I could help students internalize the transformative power of reading and writing. My concerns about engaging students in meaningful learning led to my writing *Engaging Adolescent Learners* (2006), in which I adapted Brian Cambourne's Conditions of Learning, typically used with young children, for use in secondary classrooms.

Then, as a literacy coordinator at the University of Central Florida, I added another component that I now feel is foundational to learning: community. I discovered that, whether working with young children, resistant adolescents, or weary teachers, community is essential to the deep and sustained learning that is often lacking in traditional, textbook-based classrooms. That realization led me to write another book, *Literacy Learning Communities: A Guide for Sustainable Change in Secondary Schools* (2007).

But it was not until I was struggling with a chapter on "deep reading" while writing *Literacy for Real: Reading, Thinking, and Learning in the Content Areas* (2009) that I was introduced to Jimmy. I was trying to contrast ways students read various texts, such as a cartoon, a graph, and a poem; I had found a great example of a cartoon and graph, but I couldn't find just the right poem. I was familiar with Jimmy's poetry and I knew that teens found his poems easy to access and yet profoundly moving, so I looked through a few of his books of poetry. Finally, I found a poem that I felt would be perfect for the chapter, but I thought the permissions fee to reprint it might be too steep. So I kept plugging in different poems—but each one dimmed against the shadow of Jimmy's poem.

Finally, I decided to contact Jimmy and make my case for a reasonable fee. We came to an agreement and, in gratitude, I sent Jimmy a copy of my book *Engaging Adolescent Learners*. A few weeks later, I received an email from him asking if we could talk about some educational work he was doing with his nonprofit organization, Cedar Tree. But first, he asked that I read his memoir, *A Place to Stand* (2002), so I would know more about who he was and how he came to love reading and writing.

I read Jimmy's gripping, transcendent story in one huge gulp, holding my breath for hours on end, it seemed, even though I knew the outcome. But it was his connection with language, with literacy, that brought tears to my eyes.

> Language was opening me up in ways I couldn't explain and I assumed it was part of the apprenticeship of a poet. I culled poetry from odors, sounds, faces, and ordinary events occurring around me. Breezes bulged me as if I were cloth; sounds nicked their marks on my nerves; objects made impressions on my sight as if in clay. There, in the soft lightning of language, life centered and ground itself in me and I was flowing with the grain of the universe. Language placed my life experiences in a new context, freeing me for the moment to become with air as air, with clouds as clouds, from which new associations arose to engage me in present life in a more purposeful way. (2001, 240)

I remember clearly the day Jimmy and I finally connected by phone. Our mutual enthusiasm and commitment to reading, writing, and most of all, adolescents, created such synergy that the wires seemed to buzz. He told me that the ideas in my book were right in line with his philosophy about education and his ongoing literacy work with prisoners and students. I was intrigued that this poet not only felt my passion for education but experienced it so deeply that he was devoting his life to it.

Jimmy embraces new ideas with an immediacy and fervor that leaves no room for hesitation so, before I knew it, we had plans—big plans—to work together and write a book that would fuse Jimmy's talents as a writer of memoir with my experience in engaging communities of learners. With every conversation, we became more convinced that we could contribute to the national movement in adolescent literacy in a way that leaves behind notions of coercing learning through standardized tests or forcing teachers to rely on scientifically based programs that take students lockstep through levels of achievement. The short of it was that we felt that our collaboration, based on the approach we advocate in this book, could foment a revolution in adolescent learning.

The Intended Audience for This Book

This is a book for reading coaches, teachers, principals, and district staff who have good students who need to be challenged, students who are unmotivated, students at risk of dropping out, or students who are learning English as a second language. *Adolescents on the Edge* is a model for a new *way* of learning that includes providing texts that resonate with students and then using such texts to create communities that transcend the stereotypes and frustrations that dog many classrooms.

We are not alone in our vision, of course. Paige Kuni, past chair of the Partnership for 21st Century Skills, for example, noted, "Learning supports are only valuable if they effectively reinforce human relationships, give relevance to learning and encourage student engagement" (Kuni 2009). Clearly, we agree with these statements, but agreement can be miles from implementation. Such an approach, as with most things that really matter, will take time. But we believe that beginning now, *today*, teachers, administrators, and states can commit to reinforcing relationships, providing relevant learning texts and tasks, and encouraging student engagement. Our intent with this book is to show readers explicitly how to make these things happen.

How to Use This Book

This book is a new type of professional development tool, written for active use with students in classrooms. There are several components, which together create a package that will enable you to immerse your students in quality literature and that can become a springboard for effective instructional practices.

- the teacher's edition
- the DVD that accompanies the teacher's book
- the student edition, *Stories from the Edge*, which can be purchased separately

The Teacher's Edition

The first six chapters provide a description of what we believe are the most important elements in creating transformative learning along with suggestions for classroom implementation.

We begin with how to create a community in your classroom through trust and dialogue. From there, we offer researched practices for engaging and motivating your students. We address the importance of self-efficacy and challenging tasks, again with explicit suggestions for incorporating these components into your instruction. The last three chapters are even more practical, showing readers how to use Jimmy's stories, as well as other texts, as the basis for group work, writing, reading, speaking, listening, and project-based learning. Although suggestions for teaching and sample lessons appear after each of Jimmy's stories in Part 2 of the book, we also use his stories as examples for instructional practices in these first six chapters. Everything we offer comes with the understanding that community is the foundation on which all instruction is built.

The second half of the book contains new stories that Jimmy wrote especially for adolescents. The stories are based on Jimmy's early life growing up in an orphanage and on his adult life since he was released from prison. The stories are grouped into three sections by overarching themes: "Longing for Love," "Stereotypes," and "Wholeness." In these stories, Jimmy doesn't preach, he doesn't insist—he merely offers his truth in ways that, like art, mirrors everyone's reality. With the accompanying lessons, students are led to explore their own truths and, perhaps more importantly, to come to trust the power of literacy.

The DVD

When we first began this book, I wanted students (and their teachers) to have an opportunity to actually hear and see Jimmy. I wanted them to experience the power of his words and the conviction with which he speaks about issues that are life-altering. I wanted them to know that literature is more than just pieces of text with comprehension questions following, and most of all, I wanted them to know that they, like Jimmy, have something to say. Thankfully, this DVD soon became more than just my desire.

Viewing Jimmy's Stories

These segments of the DVD allow teachers and their students to "sit in" as Jimmy tells his stories to a group of adolescents. Suddenly, the stories are not merely words on a page; they are alive—the way stories are meant to be experienced. A master storyteller, Jimmy weaves threads of tales that can be tragic, funny, exciting, poignant—often all at the same time. But it is not only the narrative that will hook students, because his stories are intended to do more than entertain. Jimmy's convictions will move them to introspection. His insistence that every single person can make choices, even under the most horrendous circumstances, will empower them to believe that they, too, can succeed. Most of all, Jimmy's unrelenting mantra, that literacy is freedom, and that everyone who is breathing has something significant to say, will inspire both students and teachers.

Viewing the Lessons

After the stories, teachers and students can watch the lessons that follow. Watching Jimmy and I working with real adolescents will give you ideas for discussion and writing. Read How to Use the DVD with Your Students and Colleagues on page 162 for more specific activities and suggestions to use with each video clip.

Watching the video with others on your grade level or team can turn the experience into a study lesson. "In this format, teachers examine their practice to answer questions about how they can increase their students' learning by selecting an overarching goal and related research question they want to explore. They then work collaboratively on creating 'study lessons' where they draw up a detailed plan for the lesson. One of the teachers uses the lesson in a real classroom as other members observe. The group comes back together to discuss their observations" (Lent 2007, 128).

Finally, teachers can enjoy watching an informal dialogue as Jimmy and I discuss classroom practices with other teachers. This segment may be the basis for further reflection with colleagues.

The Student Edition

All the stories in the teacher's edition are included in a separate student edition, *Stories from the Edge*, so that students have easy access to the texts. The student book also contains three *additional* new stories by Jimmy that will draw kids in and keep them there, which you can use in your classroom or simply let students read independently: a hilarious story about a stubborn dog, Teddy, who insists on being part of a sacred ceremony; Jimmy's reminiscence about the time he was trying to keep his car from being repossessed; and a story about working with a group of tough young felons in a prison setting.

As I reflect on this book, I return to that cold day in Milwaukee and remember my absolute certainty that literacy within community is a fundamental part of the answer that has for so long eluded us. Now a decade into the twenty-first century, we must reevaluate sophisticated-sounding terms, such as "response to intervention" or "adequate yearly progress" and truly go back to the basics: quality texts, honest dialogue, intrinsic motivation, and a belief that, *together*, adults and students can discover how to transform learning from "work" done in school into memorable, interactive experiences that will stay with them forever.

The authors and publisher wish to thank those who have generously given permission to reprint borrowed material:

"Model of Learning" from *The Whole Story* by Brian Cambourne. Copyright © 1988 by Brian Cambourne. Published by Scholastic Inc. Reprinted by permission of the publisher.

"I Am with Those"; "Jewelry Store"; and "The Handsome World" from *Immigrants in Our Own Land* by Jimmy Santiago Baca. Copyright © 1979 by Jimmy Santiago Baca. Published by New Directions Publishing Corp. Reprinted by permission of the publisher.

"Ancestors Run Next to Me" and "Spring Arrives" from *Spring Poems Along the Rio Grande* by Jimmy Santiago Baca. Copyright © 2007 by Jimmy Santiago Baca. Published by New Directions Publishing Corp. Reprinted by permission of the publisher.

Excerpts from "An Interview with Santiago Baca" by Frederick Luis Aldama originally appeared in *MELUS: Journal of the Society for the Study of the Multi-Ethnic Literature of the United States*, issue 30.3 (Fall 2005), pages 113–27. Reprinted by permission of the publisher.

Excerpts from "Jimmy Santiago Baca Interview" by Barbara Stahura originally appeared in *The Progressive*, January 2006, Volume 67, No. 1. Reprinted by permission of the publisher.

Excerpts from " 'Sucked into a Shooting Star': A Conversation with Jimmy Santiago Baca" by Jean Cheney originally appeared in *Human Ties, Utah Humanities Council Newsletter*, Fall 2009. Reprinted by permission of the Utah Humanities Council.

Excerpts from "Interview with Jimmy Santiago Baca" by Elizabeth Farnsworth from *The NewsHour with Jim Lehrer*, August 9, 2001. Copyright © 2001 by MacNeil/Lehrer Productions. Reprinted by permission of MacNeil/Lehrer Productions.

Reaching and Teaching Adolescents on the Edge

Community and Trust

But more than my fear, is my love of justice,
more than my pride is to step aside
when someone is right.

—Jimmy Santiago Baca, "I Am with Those"

In an alternative school I recently visited, I asked one of the teachers about his goals for the students. I was surprised by his candor and dismayed by his answer.

"My goal is to keep their heads down."

His reply explained the stacks of worksheets, long lists of vocabulary words, and various multiple-choice tests that lined the counter. These students may gain the necessary credits to graduate, but will they be educated? They will miss a unique opportunity to legitimize their learning by sharing ideas, participating in discussions, asking questions, responding to challenges, and engaging in countless other intellectual pursuits that flourish within a community of learners.

Learning through community has become an educational mainstay in recent years, from professional learning communities for teachers to collaborative learning for students. The Partnership for 21st Century Skills emphasizes learning and thinking that include not only traditional critical thinking and problem-solving skills but also communication and collaboration. It is noteworthy that the vision of the partnership includes behaviors that are essential for communal learning, such as leadership, adaptability, personal responsibility, people skills, and social responsibility. In a recent article in the *Christian Science Monitor*, the author reinforces this concept.

"In a knowledge economy . . . the ability to articulate and solve problems, to generate original ideas, and to work collaboratively across cultural boundaries is growing exponentially in importance" (Khadaroo 2009). These social and personal skills will not develop in isolation. Students' heads must be up and they must be actively involved in their communities, including communities created in school.

The advantages of communal learning are hard to ignore. Teachers working in community report increased morale, lower absenteeism, and sustained, transferable learning. Adolescents say that they work harder, find school more interesting, and skip class less often when they are allowed to work collaboratively. This research has led to the creation of smaller schools, academies, and magnet programs, but interestingly, when schools were only smaller in number of students and lacked the critical components of "community, intellectual and personal engagement, authentic learning and assessment, and trusting relationships among adults and students," there were no advantages over larger schools (Ancess 2008, 49).

These findings are not surprising. Although students have obvious academic requirements, their emotional and social needs are enormous. It is through community that they learn not only to respect others but to find respect for themselves. They learn how to disagree with each other while attempting to understand and have empathy for those who have different views, essential skills for their futures in a global setting.

Relationships, the key component for successful communities, must be nurtured and given time to develop, but they will never form if the members of a class are not offered the opportunity to know one another beyond the superficial. Jimmy's stories encourage community because they address our deepest hungers and frailties: the desire to belong, the tendency to stereotype others, the need for unconditional love, the tension between who we are and who we want to become. Through relationships with others we begin to unravel these layered, complex issues that define our own humanity.

How to Build Trust

Because the stories in this book will challenge students to think about themselves and others in new ways, students must feel safe to explore and then express what they think, feel, or believe. Indeed, efficient learning cannot take place when the learner is experiencing fear or stress (Goswami 2008). The best antidote for such anxiety is an environment where students trust each other and their teachers. When trust is present in a community, there is a palpable shift in the quality of conversations and depth of understanding.

This is all very different from traditional classrooms where the teacher asks questions and students try to find the "right" answers in order to be rewarded with a good grade. In a trusting environment, students feel free to take intellectual and emotional risks while learning about social boundaries. At first, the trust may be tentative, but it will evolve when relationships are valued and students are confident that they will not suffer indignities, embarrassment, or ridicule when they put themselves out there.

In her book *Trust Matters: Leadership for Successful Schools*, Megan Tschannen-Moran (2004) has identified five facets essential for trust to occur. These elements also have strong implications for trust within the classroom:

- *benevolence*: caring, support, expressing appreciation, and being fair
- *honesty*: integrity, telling the truth, keeping promises, being real
- *openness*: sharing power, decision making, and important information
- *reliability*: consistency, dependability, diligence
- *competence*: engaging in problem solving, fostering conflict resolution, and working hard

Many adolescents may be afraid to trust because they have been let down so often or they may have had to rely on themselves and have had few positive experiences with trust. Provide a copy of Tschannen-Moran's facets of trust to students and invite them to examine each in light of their own experience. Ask them if there are other components of trust that Tschannen-Moran could have included. Then, use the following questions to initiate a discussion with your students or as writing prompts to help you understand their individual levels of trust.

- Have you experienced fair treatment, either by family or by the system?
- How do you express appreciation? Do you often receive appreciation for your acts?
- How important is it for promises to be kept, either those made to you or those you make to others?
- Do you feel that you are a part of decision making that affects your life?

- Are you dependable? Do you feel others are dependable?
- How do you generally resolve conflicts?
- How important is truthfulness to you?

Be forthright in telling students that you hope to create a community within the class and that students must address issues such as these in honest ways to build a foundation for examining other, more complex issues that they will read about in Jimmy's stories.

How to Build Community

A community, like any single relationship, is not static. It may be airtight one day—blood brothers (or sisters) forever—and in ruins the next, perhaps because of a rift that seems too deep to overcome. The goal is to keep the relationships among members of the community strong enough so that they grow from both the highs and lows of interpersonal experiences. In a classroom setting, you can be like the calm and objective therapist helping your clients maintain equilibrium as they move forward in relationship. While every teacher knows that there will be good days and not-so-good days, it is through the *process* of building community that students will gain life-altering skills. Fortunately, Jimmy's stories will help you with this process as they provide the raw material for building and sustaining a community in your class.

Invite Students In

In Alfred Tatum's research (2009) with African American adolescent males, he notes that becoming a better teacher begins by inviting students' voices into the process. From the very beginning, create an environment where students know what to expect and are a part of setting those expectations. For example, allow students to set ground rules, or guiding principles, for interaction, such as "Only one person speaks at a time" or "Disagreeing with someone's idea is okay; attacking someone over what they believe is not." Begin by asking students what is most important when they speak or listen to someone and go from there.

Have a student record the principles the class adopts on chart paper and post the rules so there is no confusion about expectations. Show students that you will be fair in demanding that everyone adhere to the principles for discussion and behavior that *they* created. The rules may change as the community develops and respect becomes the guiding principle.

As much as possible, try to create a classroom that belongs to the students. Here are some ways to do that:

- Give students folders to hold their writing and an accessible space to keep the folders inside the class.
- Put an artistic student (or team) in charge of creating bulletin boards to display student poetry, writing, or art associated with the stories they have read.
- Allow students to write quotes from the stories (or other texts) on the board when they find a line that is especially appealing.
- Whenever possible, allow students to collectively make decisions about classroom procedures, schedules, or assignments.

When students believe that the space in which they learn is *theirs*, they will work together to maintain it, building community along the way.

Create Common Goals

Community is formed when people have common goals and a vested interest in attaining those goals. Look for opportunities to help students form goals by arranging activities outside of the classroom that will allow them to work together. In a study of five California high schools that "have beaten the odds in supporting the success of low-income students of color," the researchers noted that "schools connect students to their communities and their futures through community service, internships, and partnerships with community groups and colleges" (Darling-Hammond and Friedlander 2008, 15).

After each story, we have provided a section titled "Beyond the Classroom" to help transfer learning to out-of-school settings. For example:

- As you use the stories to help students write, and as students begin to polish their work for an audience, you may arrange for a poetry reading or storytelling event at a local café.
- Arrange for students to read their pieces to the elderly or elementary school children.

- Students might form a book club during lunch and read Jimmy's life story, *A Place to Stand*, one of his many books of poetry, or young adult novels with which they may identify, such as those by Sharon Draper or Walter Dean Myers.

- Encourage students to think beyond the classroom to make literacy relevant and purposeful by engaging in community service projects.

See Chapter 6, "Performances and Projects," for more information on this topic.

Model the Behaviors of Strong Relationships

Recognize that forming community, especially with students who may not have experienced many close relationships in their lives, is a leap of faith. But reliable relationships with their teacher and peers can make a significant difference for all adolescents. Sonia Nieto in her book *The Light in Their Eyes* (1999) reported that "Mexican American tenth graders from similar social class backgrounds sought to determine why some of them were successful academically while others were not. A major finding of the study was that a supportive network of teachers and friends was linked to the academic success of students" (99).

Students must know without doubt that you know them, care about them, and believe in them. Address each student by name both in and outside of your class, ask how things are going, and try to talk in specifics when you're aware of important events in students' lives. Smile, even when you're tired. The fascinating research on mirror neurons, neurons in an observer's brain that fire when she sees someone else perform a similar act, "might provide the same powerful unifying framework for our understanding of teaching and learning that the discovery of DNA did for our understanding of genetics" (Sylwester 2008, 29).

Richard Restak, neurologist, explains it by saying, "When we watch another person move, our observation of the movement activates those areas in our brain that we would use if we moved the same way" (2008, 7). That understanding allows us to enhance the behavior of our students by modeling what we want them to mimic, such as empathy, respect, caring—or happiness. More important, however, is the fact that such behaviors strengthen bonds with students, create a positive environment, and, over time, allow trusting relationships to develop.

Modeling behaviors that underlie strong relationships is especially important if you have a student who is disruptive or difficult. Alfred Tatum notes that there are several guideposts useful for literacy as collaborative acts. One of those is "exhibiting caring" and the other is what he calls "reflecting before rejecting"—dealing with immature or unacceptable behavior by talking through an issue rather than responding with rejection (Tatum 2009). The idea is that you deal with a difficult student just as you would respond to anyone with whom you have a strong relationship.

- Speak firmly but kindly.
- Express caring even though you may be upset or angry.
- Practice honesty in all communication.
- Use reason instead of pulling rank.
- Apologize later if you say something you wish you hadn't said.

Although these behaviors may be difficult to practice, it is extremely important for students to observe how one person deals with another within relationship when there is conflict or disagreement. It may be reassuring to know that Jimmy and I have found when community bonds are strong, volatile situations and inappropriate behavior often diminish or disappear altogether.

Many of Jimmy's stories center around conflicts that will provide students with wonderful opportunities to ponder what they would do under the same circumstances, what they would expect from another person, or what they think is best to do. Chapter 6 offers role-playing activities that may help students get outside themselves long enough to objectify their feelings about some of the events in Jimmy's stories that may strike close to home. The short of it is that, as the community leader, you have a huge responsibility and a unique opportunity to show students how relationships work to build community in the classroom and within their extended lives.

Foster Dialogue

Members of a community spend a lot of time talking with each other, and it is such dialogue that increases understanding and cements relationships. Chapter 4 addresses ways of creating group discussion and reinforces the role that dialogue plays in building community and trust.

With each story, we have provided prompts for discussion because we know the value of communication as a bridge to relationship. It is through such discussion that students come to know the threads of each other's lives and their resultant values. In many schools, teachers avoid "dangerous discourses," discussions that challenge students' accepted social ideologies. It will be nearly impossible to use Jimmy's stories effectively if you are not willing to invite discourse that may, at times, feel risky. As Sonia Nieto notes, "Paradoxically, it is precisely these 'dangerous discourses' that appeal to many students, particularly those who live daily with the realities that such discourses uncover. Encouraging these kinds of conversations is a message to students that the classrooms belong to them also because they are places where meaningful dialogue can occur around issues that are central to students' lives" (1999, 120–21). Once students feel safe to express themselves, the discourse will become authentic, allowing the full examination of issues that may have fermented under layers of stereotypes, misperceptions, or self-doubt.

Sometimes it is best not to rush immediately into dialogue, however. Allow students time and space to process their thoughts individually before asking them to share with others. Writing is one way students can do this, especially if you let them know beforehand that sharing is not required. Also, resist the urge to have students answer "comprehension" questions about what they have read, although it may be helpful to provide "thinking prompts," such as "What would you have done if you had been in a similar situation?" or "What would you say to (a certain character) about his actions if you were his friend?" In any case, encourage students to use learning logs or journals for responses, questions, sketches, jot lists, or freewriting. If you are asking students to share their thoughts, let them do this initially with a partner and then with a small group rather than facilitating a whole-class discussion immediately. "Reporters" can offer summaries from individual group discussions with the reassurance that others in the group will "have his back." In a relatively short amount of time, you will find that dialogue not only will help students process what they have read but also will lead to increased trust and a more solid community.

Engage in Community-Building Activities

People who are part of a community share the events of their lives and cheer for each other's accomplishments. Here are some ways you can do this in your classroom:

- Post a calendar and write each student's birthday on the appropriate date.

- Encourage students to report on the good things they know about each other.

- Celebrate positive events and achievements.

- Allow a few minutes at the beginning of each period for student announcements.

- Attend extracurricular events, such as basketball games or plays, when students in your class participate in these activities. Although you, as the teacher, may not always be available to attend, encourage members of the class to support each other by going, perhaps as a group.

The benefits of community also increase when people engage in enjoyable activities together. For example:

- Allow students to bring food for in-class performances or when they read silently.

- Give them social time to simply talk with each other, perhaps the first or last five minutes of class.

- Create bulletin boards for students to post photographs, announcements, ideas, or responses to the stories.

- Have a digital camera handy to capture moments that define community.

An accepting and secure environment that offers a variety of social and intellectual activities allows students to truly know each other, beginning the cycle of trust, loyalty, relationship, and enduring community.

Further Reading

Community: the Structure of Belonging (Block 2008)
The Freedom Writer's Diary (Gruwell, Filopivic, and Freedom Writers 1999)
The Light in Their Eyes: Creating Multicultural Learning Communities (Nieto 1999)
Reading for Their Life: (Re) Building Textual Lineages of African American Males (Tatum 2009)

2

Engagement and Motivation

I stand up, grass all around me, and start
walking through the tall grass, listening to myself live,
hearing my foot lift and set, lift and set, carrying me
like a stray animal, a holy one who rose out of mud, with mind
of man, heart of earth, taking my body-form as others,
from now on, I scream and howl and love and laugh, I am me.

—Jimmy Santiago Baca, "The Handsome World"

During the twentieth century, *engagement and motivation* was not a term found in most secondary school improvement plans, state standards, or on faculty meeting agendas. Some students may have been more inherently motivated to study certain subjects than others, but that was beside the point. There was X amount of work to be done to pass a course and, engaged or not, students were expected to complete the assignments. The threat of receiving an F usually did the trick because, for the most part, students cared if they failed.

Enter the twenty-first century and behold a generation like none we've ever seen before. Dubbed the M (multitasking) or N (net) Generation, these kids don't stand still. Suddenly, engagement in *life* is the name of the game with intrinsic motivation built in—video games, Wii, text-messaging, MySpace. These same students, highly engaged in out-of-school literacies, often don't seem to be able to focus on in-school texts or assignments. It should come as no surprise to anyone paying attention that the dropout rate would climb in this new century, especially for African Americans (55.3 percent), Hispanics (57.8 percent), and Native Americans (50.6 percent) (Editorial Projects in Education 2008).

With a scare rivaling the stock market tumble, policy makers could no longer ignore the fact that many American adolescents were in serious trouble educationally. The United States ranked fifteenth out of twenty-nine OECD (Organisation for Economic Cooperation and Development) countries in reading literacy in 2003, the last year for which data are available. Then, in 2006, the United States fell to twenty-first and twenty-fifth of thirty OECD countries in scientific literacy and math literacy respectively (Wise 2009). Respected educational and research organizations such as the Alliance for Excellent Education and the Florida Center for Reading Research began publishing documents with the words *motivation* and *engagement* front and center. In a publication titled "Adolescents and Literacy: Reading for the 21st Century," for example, the author notes "Motivation is one concept that continually surfaces as an important focus in reading and learning to read, particularly for adolescents" (Kamil 2003, 2).

The Center on Instruction published a similar document on adolescent literacy and included as one of five areas of instructional focus and improvement "increasing the use of a variety of practices to increase motivation and engagement with reading" (Torgesen et al. 2007, 16). In 2005, the North Central Regional Educational Laboratory (NCREL) created an action guide titled "Using Student Engagement to Improve Adolescent Literacy," which cites studies that show academic achievement increasing when associated with engagement in reading and classroom-related activities for virtually all racial/ethnic groups.

Despite such compelling research, teachers with whom Jimmy and I work often become discouraged or overwhelmed when we mention engagement. They tell us they have enough to do in the course of a day without making sure students are *engaged*, a word they sometimes mistake for *entertained*. In fact, it is not the teachers' responsibility to keep students engaged, but rather to provide relevant and meaningful text, assignments, and opportunities for learning that will foster engagement as a natural byproduct. Students who are engaged in learning seek to understand new information because they find it relevant and useful to their lives.

Cambourne's Conditions for Learning as a Model of Engagement

Brian Cambourne, head of the Centre for Studies in Literacy at Wollongong University in Australia, has studied engagement for more than thirty years, and he places it as the bull's-eye of all learning. His model, Cambourne's conditions of learning, makes clear that students must perceive a need or purpose for learning, must actively participate in learning, and must have a safe environment in which to try out or "approximate" learning.

Figure 2–1 is a visual representation of Cambourne's model of learning from my book on engagement, *Engaging Adolescent Learners: A Guide for Content-Area Teachers* (2006). The conditions of learning, as outlined by Cambourne, can be adapted to any setting, but they are especially important when working with adolescents who have not previously been successful in school or who have other issues with learning. Giving students more of the same, no matter how beautifully wrapped the package, will not fool kids who have spent their educational careers feeling displaced, disengaged, and discouraged. There must be a change in how we as teachers approach teaching as well as how students perceive learning, and the change begins with engagement.

Immersion

According to Cambourne, learners must be "saturated by, enveloped in, flooded by, steeped in, or constantly bathed in that which is to be learned" (Cambourne 1995, 185). For adolescents immersed in Jimmy's stories and poems, that means they must be presented with all types of experiences that allow them to read, write, talk, and think about text. Jimmy and I have found students intensely motivated by his stories, and the accompanying lessons will allow them to tap into this engagement while honing their literacy skills.

One of our goals with both the stories and lessons is to help students experience *flow*, a condition coined by Mihaly Csikszentmihalyi, the author of several books on the topic. In a 2002 interview, he explains that to experience flow one must balance skills and challenges so that he or she begins to forget everything bothersome in everyday life, including "the self as an entity separate from what was going on." The participant or learner is a part of something greater and is "moving along with the logic of the activ-

FIGURE 2-1

Cambourne's Model of Learning

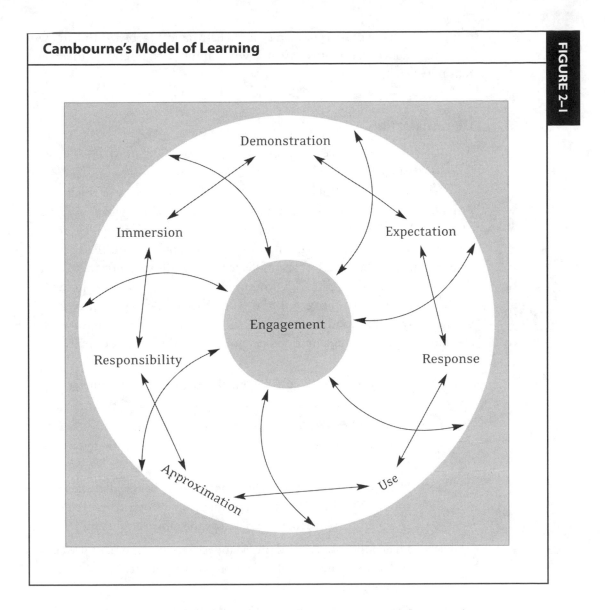

ity" (Debold 2002). Certainly our students have experienced flow on the basketball court, while playing music, or even when involved in a project at school that is relevant and interesting to them. But how many students have experienced flow when reading a poem, writing about an event in their life, or discussing an idea they had never considered before? After students read about the young Jimmy trying to steal a glass eye from a man he describes as "a grizzly ogre, with Popeye forearms, hair stiff and bristly as barbwire, a permanent scowl on his face, and a perennial stream of yellowish mucus dripping from the glass eye socket" in "The Magic Marble," students will fall into quiet contemplation as they write about a character of their own that may rival Jimmy's.

Demonstration

Another of Cambourne's conditions for learning is demonstration, where learners "observe (see, hear, witness, experience, feel, study, explore) actions and artifacts" (Cambourne 1995, 187). The stories in this volume provide a natural vehicle for demonstrating literacy skills within a context of quality literature. Show students how you, as a proficient reader, process what you are reading by engaging in "think-alouds" as you read some of Jimmy's stories aloud to the class. This technique allows students to eavesdrop on your "reading mind" as you unlock text. For example, in the following excerpt from "Forgiving the Godfather of Poetry" notice how a teacher may think aloud as she reads, showing students that mature readers may have conflicting emotions or thoughts as they consider text.

TEXT: "I got up and walked a few blocks to the Camden cemetery where I found Walt's grave."

TEACHER: I wonder how Walt Whitman's grave is marked. He's such a famous poet; I would think there would be a big statue or gravestone.

TEXT: "Sitting next to it, I thought about how he believed in the doctrine of Manifest Destiny, that America was destined, even ordained by God, to expand across the entire continent."

TEACHER: I remember studying about Manifest Destiny in one of my classes, but I was never really clear on what it meant. I need to look it up online.

TEXT: "Many of my people, Native American Mexicans, indigenous Mexicans, tribal Mexicans with roots plunging deep into pre–Columbian times, were hanged, burned out, murdered, raped, and driven off their lands in the name of this doctrine."

TEACHER: I never, ever, realized that the Doctrine was used as an excuse for murder! How could I have missed this when I was in school? I wonder if the textbooks leave out this part? I really want to know more about this.

Of course you wouldn't reflect to such an extent after each line, but it is very helpful for students who may be struggling with reading skills to hear how you think through ideas in print—and that it is okay to read slowly, even stopping to think along the way.

One caution: Students may want to jump into a discussion of the content as you read or express your thoughts, but insist that they simply listen. Point out that each reader has the right to think what he or she wants while reading—without interference from anyone else—one of the great liberties of silent reading.

Expectations

Students seem to have built-in antennae that work very well in helping them know the expectations others have of them. In some cases, there is no need to use that special feeler because the expectations are tragically apparent. Labeling students based on standardized test scores, treating them as if they can't be trusted, speaking to them in a harsh, demeaning way, and a thousand other words and actions, both positive and negative, cement expectations, often for years in the future. As Cambourne notes, expectations are "subtle and powerful coercers of behavior" (1995, 187) and, Jimmy and I would add, of learning.

In Chapter 1 we suggest that students create ground rules for discussions, a type of expectation-setting activity. By allowing students to come up with rules for their own behavior, you are demonstrating your confidence in them and helping them learn to set realistic expectations. Other activities that will help in this area include the following.

- Have students keep a portfolio of their work and review it with them periodically. Point out how they have improved in specific areas, and ask them what more they expect of themselves, instead of telling them what they should do.

- Have students write literacy goals for themselves, for example, "I will write once each day in my journal after school" or "I will read at least one book each month." Help them create a way to monitor their progress and encourage them to share it with you or others in the class, such as writing partners.

- Use writing prompts for revision that don't focus on deficits, such as "What details could you add to make your writing more specific?" or

"How could you revise your story to make your character walk off of the page?"

The key to helping students with their own expectations is to come to know each of them well so that they trust you when you express confidence in their abilities. Recall that engagement can be experienced as flow. One of the secrets of flow is to engage in tasks that are sufficiently challenging but not so difficult that they are frustrating, often called the "zone of proximal development" (Vygotsky1978). As you learn what your students are capable of doing, you will be better able to help them achieve their own flow by setting reasonable expectations. Many students have lived with such low expectations of themselves and their peers that it may take time for a shift in understanding of their abilities, but celebrating successes and honoring students for their own unique talents will soon evolve into self-fulfilling prophecies.

Responsibility

As teachers, our mantras are often variations of the responsibility theme: students should take more responsibility for their learning, their homework, their *lives*. We may forget that taking responsibility means making decisions. When we make all the decisions for our students—what they read, what they write, what questions they answer, who they work with— we are denying them opportunities to learn how to take responsibility. Cambourne writes that learners must be "permitted to make some decisions about what they'll engage with and what they'll ignore." They must decide "when, how, and what 'bits' to learn in any learning task. Learners who lose the ability to make decisions are disempowered" (1995, 185).

Because we each individually develop our own schema, the unique set of experiences, emotions, and information that we have stored in our minds, it may be challenging to know which story will resonate with which student. For example, students whose families may have had their car repossessed will bring their own background knowledge to "Repo Man" (found in *Stories from the Edge*). Such knowledge will color how they relate to the story. To expect every person to have the same reaction, to find the same theme, or to come away from the reading with the same understanding is to deny human nature and to disallow students the opportunity to take responsibility for their own learning (Rosenblatt 2005). In fact, such expectations teach students that they don't need to assume responsibility; someone else will eventually do it for them.

The lessons included with each story offer multiple opportunities for student choice. The following practices may also be helpful when students approach the text.

- Allow students opportunities to choose their writing partners and discussion groups. It is fine for you to set parameters, however, such as "You must change partners once a week" or "If you become disruptive, I have the option of moving you to another group." Make sure students understand that you will rearrange groups if students are not holding up their end of the bargain, but send a clear message that they are capable of making choices and, within reason, you will honor those choices.

- Give up control over what doesn't really matter. For example, have the class vote on project due dates and allow students to decide what they will research related to the stories or the genre in which they will write.

- If students do not complete their work or are consistently late, refuse to accept the assignment until they write a letter to you explaining the delay. Remember that the point is to foster responsibility, so be generous in your acceptance, writing a brief note back to the student, asking that he or she explain further if you sense dishonesty or avoidance.

- Ask students to assume classroom tasks, such as facilitating group discussions, recording brainstorming ideas, or deciding how the room should be arranged for various activities. Consider committees within the class, such as a curriculum committee, project committee, or social committee, all with specific responsibilities.

When we allow students to become responsible, our job becomes lighter. Middle and high school students are capable of much more than we usually expect of them, and they will never learn just how much they *can* do until we relinquish a bit of control. For too long, American teachers have been giving the proverbial fish instead of teaching students to fish for life.

Approximation

Cambourne notes that "approximation," making errors in learning as a part of the process, is a condition that teachers understand but find difficult to implement in the classroom (1988, 66). That comes as no surprise since our definition of learning, at least according to policymakers, is defined by the results of standardized tests that offer little room for error. This is no small oversight, since Cambourne found the "freedom to approximate" an "essential ingredient in all successful learning" (1995, 185). As discussed in Chapter 1, learners must feel safe to approximate learning, that is, to take risks and make mistakes as an important part of the *process* of understanding. Approximation is "synonymous with the process of hypothesis, inquiry, and discovery: trying first one educated guess, learning as much from the guess as from the success, and moving in total absorption to deeper learning. Without the freedom to inquire as a natural part of learning, the imposed ceiling may have long-lasting effects on learners' confidence in their intellectual abilities as well as on their ambition to try anything that does not come with an assurance of success" (Lent 2006, 90).

Fortunately, Jimmy's stories have within them the seeds of approximation, as they show students how mistakes can be turned into important learning opportunities. Indeed, Jimmy's life story is a shining example of approximation—teaching himself to read and write after his mistakes led him to a five-year sentence in a federal prison. It was only after many false starts that these experiences eventually allowed him to write award-winning poetry. Through such personal narratives, students will come to embrace rather than fear mistakes, understanding that they are opportunities for growth and readjustment, signaling the beginning of hope and optimism instead of the final death knell.

Use Jimmy's stories to engage students in ongoing discussions of how mistakes can be vital for increased learning. The following prompts for students can be used to guide the dialogue or writing sessions.

- Think about something you learned to do, such as playing a musical instrument or participating in a sport. Describe mistakes you made while learning. How did the mistakes help you become better at what you were doing?

- Think about something that was easy for you to learn. What mistakes do others make while learning this activity? What advice would you give to those who are new to this field? How could their mistakes lead to increased learning?

- How have human lives, throughout history, been improved because of mistakes someone made while learning? (Allow students to research people who have made contributions to society, such as Thomas Edison, Benjamin Franklin, Santos Dumont, George Washington Carver, Marie Curie, or Alexander Graham Bell to find out how mistakes led to famous discoveries.)

- Describe a significant mistake you've made. How did it change your life? What did you learn from your mistake that led to increased understanding in other areas?

As students come to feel safe in their classroom environment, they will begin to risk new learning, sometimes in unexpected, phenomenal ways, surprising you as well as themselves. Help students experience learning as an ongoing, lifelong process where the "correct" answer may not necessarily be the most important one.

Use

Information that is not in some way relevant or useful is sterile. Bits of information may be helpful to use as a lifeline if you're ever on a trivia show, but learning that cannot be used in some way to make your life better, your insights sharper, or your goals closer is impotent. We understand why kids ask, "Why do I need to know this?" and if we don't have a valid answer, perhaps they really don't need to know it.

Adolescents will engage in literacy when they find it purposeful. Watch them avidly read driver's license manuals, video game instructions, or a text message from friends about what's going on this weekend. As Andrea VanderHeyden, a senior in Ontario, wrote, "I understand about learning for passion rather than just for grades. I often experience this phenomenon when I see an article as I'm surfing the Web. I'll read it and look up additional information if I'm interested even if it has nothing to do with any of my other obligations" (2008, 50). Having students read a text with the sole objective of completing a worksheet, passing a test, or gaining credit seldom fosters such engagement.

The National Research Council found that "Learners of all ages are more motivated when they can see the usefulness of what they are learning and when they can use that information to do something that has an impact on others—especially their local community" (2000, 61). With each story, Jimmy and I have provided "Beyond the Classroom" activities that tap into intrinsic motivation, activities that are both relevant and useful, but you are the best judge of what is meaningful to your own students. Use our lessons as springboards for creating your own activities, or ask students how the stories and poems could motivate them to take action.

Tell students that they will complete a project with each piece they read and ask them how the activity might be modified to be more meaningful (and still fulfill the requirements of your district or state's curriculum). For example, in "The Swing Test That Made Us Men," we suggest that students observe younger children interacting on the playground, take observational notes, and create their own story with children as main characters. This activity could be infinitely varied based on your community and the opportunities it affords. Because research shows that motivation is especially high when altruism is a part of the work, you may suggest that students become big brothers or sisters to children they meet on the playground. Your students may want to go to an elementary school and work with children in a particular classroom, creating a booklet of interviews and photographs that will be given to the class. We have seen "unmotivated" high school students spend their own time in a retirement center visiting with their elderly partner long after their English class assignment to interview the residents was completed, graded, and filed away.

If opportunities for such outside activities are unfeasible, do all you can to make the text relevant to your students by having purposeful activities before, during, and after reading. Even with a very short story such as "The Swing Test That Made Us Men," you can help create relevance with the following activities.

- Before reading: Ask students to share in small groups or with a partner a time they or a playmate got hurt on the playground as a child.
- During reading: Have students stop when they get to this line, "Breaking a bone was the symbol of manhood, a badge of courage," and write what a symbol of manhood (or womanhood) is with their peers.
- After reading: Ask each student to write one question they would like to ask Jimmy.

As Jeff Wilhelm so succinctly noted in *Engaging Readers & Writers with Inquiry*, "Without purpose, significant learning is difficult if not impossible to achieve" (2007, 8). With it, students will inherently be drawn into learning merely because it matters.

Response

While writing *Engaging Adolescent Learners*, I felt *response* was one of the most important components in engagement: "Response is a powerful force;

it can be a stimulating motivator or a suffocating inhibitor" (Lent 2006, 100). Even when the teacher ensures that all of the conditions of learning are in place, even when students assume responsibility and find the learning relevant, the lack of appropriate and caring responses from teachers can unravel the threads of engagement.

Cambourne characterizes response as *feedback* from exchanges with more knowledgeable others. What is the difference between the evaluations or assessments that so often pose as response? Cambourne explains. "While exchanges may vary in detail and richness . . . they have certain things in common: a) they are readily available, frequently given, nonthreatening and with no strings attached; b) there is no penalty for not getting the conventional form correct the next time it is produced. There is no limit to the number of exchanges that are offered and given" (1988, 40).

You will notice the close association "feedback" has with "approximation." The words "nonthreatening, no strings attached, no penalty" all confirm the importance of allowing students to try on learning as you coach from the sidelines, not offering false praise, of course, but constructive, honest feedback that shows students that you care about their progress and that you can be trusted to support them even when they are not "getting it."

For too long, teachers have been expected to "grade" attempts at learning by placing cold numbers on students' work, as if learning can be objectified in such a way. Teachers report that they are required to have a certain number of grades per marking period, but Jimmy and I believe that performance can be assessed in many ways, such as checks for participation, conference notes in portfolios, student self-assessment, and learning logs. In any event, by using the following prompts while students work on projects or assignments related to Jimmy's stories, you can hone your ability to respond—and, at the same time, help students learn how to respond to each other.

- I was wondering why you wrote about . . .
- Have you considered looking at your point from this angle?
- I'm not sure I understand why you said that. Will you explain?
- This part of your paper is brilliant—so well thought out. But toward the end you seem to lose your momentum. Can you figure out why?
- I hear what you are saying, but how does that relate to the point?
- You responded to that argument in a measured way. Can you make one last, persuasive statement?

- Your freewriting has insights that make me think. Could you distill your thoughts from this section into a poem?

- I'm trying but I really don't understand what you are saying here. Could you explain it in another way?

Responding to each other's ideas, epiphanies, or even confusion can create a community of students who come to consider their teacher and their peers valuable coaches as they fine-tune their writing, thinking, and learning.

Although research reveals that intrinsic motivation for schooling decreases as students advance through school, there is much that you can do to facilitate its rejuvenation by reminding yourself each day that your role is not to impose learning but, rather, to invite it.

Further Reading

Clock Watchers: Six Steps to Motivating and Engaging Disengaged Students Across Content Areas (Quate and McDermott 2009)

Engaging Adolescent Learners: A Guide for Content-Area Teachers (Lent 2006)

Engaging Readers & Writers with Inquiry: Promoting Deep Understanding in Language Arts and the Content Areas with Guiding Questions (Wilhelm 2007)

Challenge and Self-Efficacy

3

I rise, shivering in first-light darkness
dig deep to come up
with a prayer
enduring as the Tarahumara runner
who tops the last hill to his village at dawn.
  —Jimmy Santiago Baca, "Spring Arrives"

Booker T. Washington and Jimmy Santiago Baca have more in common than is apparent at first glance. Despite the hundred years or so that separate their births, each spent part of his life in bondage and through that experience came to understand that literacy is an essential freedom. The challenge was enormous for each man and the subsequent success was transformational, although Washington said in his autobiography *Up from Slavery* (1963), "I have learned that success is to be measured not so much by the position that one has reached in life as by the obstacles which he has had to overcome while trying to succeed."

In Jimmy's memoir, *A Place to Stand* (2002), he described the challenge of teaching himself to read and write:

> I'd study a word in connection to another word, and the longer I studied the more meanings it took on and the more subtle variations I could take from it.
>
>   I would set my dictionary next to me, prop my paper on my knees, sharpen my pencil with my teeth, and begin my reply. I would try to write the thoughts going through my mind, but they didn't come out right. . . . I erased so often and so hard I made holes in the

paper. After hours of plodding word by word to write a clear sentence, I would read it and it didn't even come close to what I'd meant to say. After a day of looking up words and writing, I'd be exhausted, as if I had run ten miles. (Baca 2001, 185)

In stark contrast to these two writers are the students that Jimmy and I visit in schools across the nation. They tell us repeatedly that they don't like to read or write, don't want to exert more effort than is required, or don't see the value in deep study. When questioned further, their response is unfailingly quick and to the point: "It's boring."

In a High School Survey of Student Engagement, Indiana University's Center for Evaluation and Education Policy surveyed thousands of students from across the United States. They asked if students had ever been bored in high school. Fifty percent of the students said they were bored every day. Their reasons? Course work that wasn't interesting, relevant, or challenging (Azzam 2008). In *"Reading Don't Fix No Chevys"* (2002), Smith and Wilhelm quote students who say that work in school is "mind numbing," although many of these students were capable of reading complicated texts on a variety of topics.

I heard the same complaints from students when I taught high school English. I also found the watered-down stories in many of the texts specifically designed for "struggling readers" to be simplistic or, as the students pointed out, "lame." Conversely, during periods of sustained silent reading, when students could choose any book from the hundreds on my classroom library shelves, they sometimes chose sophisticated novels, such as Dickey's *Deliverance*, Hansen's *The Assassination of Jesse James by the Coward Robert Ford*, or Atwood's *The Handmaid's Tale*. Others predictably choose young adult novels by Sharon Draper, Chris Crutcher, Robert Cormier, or Walter Dean Myers and devoured them, one at a time, over a few months. Some students discovered their penchant for nonfiction and read lengthy articles in *Time* or *Newsweek* about sports, medical breakthroughs, or popular culture. The choice was theirs, and they rose to levels of increasing, not decreasing, challenge.

Challenge does not exist only in text, however. As Smith and Wilhelm discovered, "We understand that the seduction of video games resides in the fact that they guarantee an appropriate challenge. As the player gets better, the game gets harder" (2006, 7). Games outside of the living room such as basketball, football, soccer, or hockey can present the same type of challenge, but notice what happens when the opposing team has a losing record. Not only is the challenge diminished, but the activities surrounding the game are anticlimactic as well. When challenge increases, engagement often soars. And challenging tasks do not equate to simply more work, as one teacher believed when she assigned her honors students double the number of tasks required of her "regular" students. The honors students spent more time doing homework, but their level of challenge did not increase.

How to Provide Challenge

Carol Ann Tomlinson, author of several books on differentiated instruction, writes that the following principles are necessary for challenge to be effective.

- The work complements students' abilities.
- The work stretches students.
- Students work hard most of the time they are in the classroom.
- Students understand they are accountable for their own growth and for contributing to the growth of others.
- Students accomplish things they didn't believe were possible. (2003, 19)

While we consider the lessons we have provided with each story challenging, only you and your students can make that determination. As Tomlinson suggests, the many factors that contribute to challenge vary according to students' individual abilities, attitudes, interests, and self-efficacy. Consider the following activities that can be used to stretch your students intellectually, potentially creating the experience of *flow*. You may alter the lessons as you create appropriate challenges for your students— that is, challenges that are not so difficult as to be frustrating, yet not so easy as to be boring.

- Chapter 6 includes ideas for student performances based on Jimmy's stories. Many students will find such activities challenging, especially if they are not accustomed to speaking in front of a group or if they feel self-conscious. It is through such activities that students learn to gain confidence and experience the satisfaction of attempting something new. Many times students get others in their group to speak for them, put their heads down to avoid the spotlight, or simply refuse to participate. Work with students one step at a time, scaffolding the process of performing, first by giving them scripted parts to read, then asking them to ad lib, and finally having them debate, role-play, or participate in a panel discussion on their own.

- Challenge students to think about issues from perspectives other than their own. For example, in the story "Eleven Cents," have students discuss whether the clerk at Wendy's was right when he didn't give Jimmy's friends a break on the eleven cents they owed because *he* had never been given a break. Listen carefully to students who side with the employee and those who side with the boys in the car. Then, ask them to defend the opposing side. Looking at a situation from a different perspective is extremely challenging but can offer the long-term reward of increased empathy and awareness of others. Barry Gilmore, in his book *Speaking Volumes: How to Get Students Discussing Books—and Much More* (2006), describes many interactive ways teachers can engage students in debates, discussions, and role-playing.

- Have students stretch or modify their innate tendencies. For example, if they write in only one genre, they will not be challenged to improve their writing or vary their thinking. While recognizing each individual's strengths, help students move beyond their comfort zone by encouraging them to try writing poetry if they usually write short stories, or to prewrite by clustering or using a jot list instead of freewriting. Challenge students to write an entire paragraph that is only one sentence or a series of sentences between four and six words long. Ask the rapper to work in iambic pentameter.

- During collaborative work, have students take on a role that is challenging for them, such as creating an illustration if they think they aren't good at art, suggesting, for example, that they create a graphic or symbolic representation instead of a realistic picture.

Challenging Thinking

Often, students are given tasks that diminish challenge because of the predictability of the assignment, such as "write an essay on this topic," "choose the correct answer," or "follow the directions." Less often are they challenged to think critically or creatively about a society over which they collectively will soon have control, what contributions they can make to the world at large, or their beliefs about how the future may look.

Asking just such questions led to an unprecedented turnout of youth in the 2008 presidential election. These young people understood that the world would soon belong to them, and that without their active participation in such issues as global warming, the economy, or civil rights, it may not be such a pretty future to inherit. It is our responsibility as teachers to ask students hard questions and empower them to think about and discuss issues that are at the core of Jimmy's stories.

- What does it mean to be whole?
- How can people with inherently different values coexist on one planet, or even in one country?
- What values will reinforce sustainability?
- How can we develop empathy and openness?
- What is justice?

At every opportunity, push students to examine their own beliefs in light of a larger, worldwide background, and encourage them to respond as active participants in this new global community, rather than as a part of the silent masses who wait for something, either good or bad, to happen to them. In the lesson for "The Warden," for example, students are asked to consider essential questions regarding the penal system, research related topics, come up with an idea for improving the system, and make a presentation to the class. Such projects give students opportunities to stretch their learning and come to believe that their ideas are worthy of consideration.

Jimmy recalls challenging a group of students during a writing workshop to take ownership of their individual gifts:

I stated emphatically that during the course of my visit, the workshop would consist of not only returning to their spiritual and creative uniqueness, showing them how to recognize their power, and advising them to use it to change the world into a better place to live for all people, but I spoke passionately on a human being's soul light and how it was theirs and should burn to brighten and illuminate the future to direct us how to live in peace. No one has the right to snuff out their creative spirit or obstruct the direction of their journey. (Baca 2009)

Critical Questioning

One of the most effective ways to help students become self-actualized learners is to introduce them to the concept of critical literacy, the idea that literacy and language can be powerful tools for personal or societal agendas. As Jimmy and I point out to students with whom we work, language has the power to transform thinking, initiate change, and reform entire structures of society and government.

In "The Journey to Be Loved," the introduction to Jimmy's stories in the second half of this book, he talks about how reading provided him "the growing capacity to think and analyze the world beyond, and to make courageous choices interacting in that world." Many students have yet to understand that by embracing literacy, they can become empowered, too, in ways they have always desired.

Part of that empowerment comes from learning how to examine online sources, print-based text, and media in general with healthy skepticism. In *Literacy for Real: Reading, Thinking and Learning in the Content Areas* (2009), I provide a chapter of activities to help students read and think critically. The process begins by teaching students how to ask questions such as the following as they read, surf the Net, or watch movies and television.

- Is the writer biased toward a particular position?
- What are the credentials of the writer?
- How reliable is the source?
- What does the writer want you to understand?
- What information might be missing?
- How would various segments of the population respond to the writer's ideas?
- Where did the writer obtain the information included in the article?
- Is the writer trying to convince the reader to believe something or to do something? If so, what and why?
- How could the information be used by different groups of people to advance their own positions?

Other questions that will challenge students to think critically include focusing on "habits of mind," such as those that Central Park East Secondary School in New York adapted for a variety of purposes:

- Evidence: How do we know?
- Viewpoint: Who is speaking?

- Connections: What causes this?
- Supposition: How might things have been different?
- Meaningfulness: What's the point? Why does it matter? (Meier 1995)

Consider using these questions as a framework for discussing Jimmy's powerful story, "Didn't Mean To," included in *Stories from the Edge*, and watch students tap into deeper intellectual and emotional responses than they may have ever experienced before.

Self-Efficacy: Seeing Themselves as Capable

Donna Alvermann doesn't mince words about the power of belief in oneself. "The potency of one's beliefs about the self is phenomenal." She goes on to explain, "In adolescence, as in earlier and later life, it is the belief in the self (or lack thereof) that makes a difference in how competent a person feels" (2003, 4). This belief about self is known as *self-efficacy*, the way an individual views his own ability to accomplish a given task (Wigfield 2004).

Self-efficacy is different from self-confidence. As teachers, we have seen plenty of kids who are loaded with self-confidence. The room lights up a notch when they enter, their very presence producing sparks, but their belief in their ability to do word problems (and their determination to try), for example, indicates a lack of self-efficacy in that particular area. Interestingly, if a math teacher can help these same kids believe they are capable of succeeding at solving word problems, their ability to do so increases. Self-efficacy is actually a predictor of success. Often students experience self-efficacy in out-of-classroom activities—basketball, for example. Their sense of capability is reinforced through crowds' adoring cheers, positive news reports in the media, and recognition by the student body. Such self-efficacy is clear and its power undeniable.

Conversely, many students who have been unsuccessful at "school" reading or writing in earlier grades have lost confidence in their ability to read or write. They have such a lack of efficacy in their own literacy abilities that they often give up before trying. We witness this phenomenon when we ask students if they are writers, and many laugh, as if the mere thought is ludicrous.

The importance of helping children gain self-efficacy while they are young cannot be overstated. I observed a fourth-grade teacher in Florida,

Jan Dykes, who turned her "writing block" into a writing workshop. One of the first things I noticed was that Jan referred to the students as "writers" and they responded as such. They enthusiastically showed me their writing notebooks, read their rough drafts aloud to me and each other, and shared their "published" pieces. Each child in this classroom experienced the power of self-efficacy; they saw themselves as writers and believed they were capable of writing. It is this type of confirmation that is missing in the lives of so many students who end up falling further and further behind because they have so few experiences that reinforce their literary abilities.

Unfortunately, the lack of self-efficacy can grow roots that spread throughout a community, creating a cycle of failure. Alfred Tatum refers to this phenomenon as "low collective self efficacy," often leading to despondency and the belief that students do not have the ability to succeed (2009). One of the most compelling aspects of Jimmy's own personal story is that he can offer these communities hope because his circumstances were, in most cases, even worse than their own, yet he overcame every obstacle that threatened to defeat him. When students see Jimmy talking in person or on the DVD about his experiences, they begin to sense hope. Here is tangible evidence that it is possible to succeed even when every marker in life points to failure, and they come to understand how Jimmy's self-efficacy played a role in his success. If *he*, a man with nothing but a desire to learn, could embrace the faintest flicker of hope and use it to pull himself from the brink of destruction, then *they*, students sitting safely in a classroom with support and resources, can make the decision to try.

How to Foster Self-Efficacy

It is naïve to suggest that you, as a teacher, are the only factor that will determine students' self-efficacy. It is realistic, however, to believe that students' experience in your class can lift them onto the first few rungs of the ladder that will give them a renewed, positive sense of self. Following are suggestions for beginning the process.

- Give students multiple opportunities to find even the smallest success in reading and writing. Use students' interests to provide text that they want to read, and ask them to share what they read with others in the class. Don't concentrate on "correct" writing, but encourage students to express themselves without worrying about spelling, punctuation, or grammar. The editing can come later in the process.

(See Chapter 5 for more information on editing.) Allow students to read their pieces to a partner, with the partner responding only to the ideas in the piece.

- When possible, publish students' writing in the school newspaper, in class booklets, or online. Send student writing home for parents to read and make it a practice to read students' work out loud to the class, anonymously, or with their names attached, with their permission. Create publishing parties where students share their poetry, short stories, or essays in an atmosphere that celebrates their efforts.

- Attempt to uncover events that may have led to students' lack of self-efficacy in literacy tasks. Lead discussions about their efforts in earlier grades that may have been less successful, and explain how specific events don't determine a setline for reading and writing.

- Involve parents in the journey. Ask students to create community literacy events where parents are invited to write with students or join a school-sponsored book club led by students.

- Create activities where students have opportunities to respond positively to their peers' intellectual efforts. For example, read a paper from an anonymous student and have other students write something that the piece prompted, or take the best lines from a set of writings and post them on the board.

Increasing students' self-efficacy often means looking at students with new eyes, seeing their potential in place of their failures. Your belief in them will transcend their negative beliefs about themselves and help them, at first haltingly and then confidently, know they are capable of using literacy skills in any way they choose.

Further Reading

Bridging the Literacy Achievement Gap, Grades 4–12 (Strickland and Alvermann, eds. 2004)

Literacy for Real: Reading, Thinking, and Learning in the Content Areas (Lent 2009)

"Reading Don't Fix No Chevys": Literacy in the Lives of Young Men (Smith and Wilhelm 2002)

4 Collaboration and Group Work

The sun strides out to track a mountain lion,
sparrows rumor about cats,
the breeze reveals herself in leaves
and steps into the river to bathe
in rippling light
—Jimmy Santiago Baca, "Ancestors Run Next to Me"

My daughter, a sophomore in college, called me recently, complaining about having to work in a group for one of her classes. Ironically, she listed many of the arguments that teachers sometimes use when they are presented with the idea of having their students engage in group activities: "I'll end up doing all the work myself—the others won't stay on task; I don't know them—it is too hard to form relationships in such a short amount of time; I don't learn as much when I work in a group; I don't have the time/energy/patience to work in a group."

Nevertheless, Kalee did spend the next few weeks working with her group on a project, and in the end, she sounded like me trying to persuade teachers of the value of group work: "I felt really good about our project. There was this artistic guy who knew a lot about photography, so he took the pictures, and another girl had this great idea. . . . We divided up the tasks. . . . I really learned from them." Not every group project turns out this positively, but more often than not, once students learn *how* to work in groups, teachers report deeper learning than when students work alone.

The Advantages of Collaboration

Research bears out these observations. Researchers have discovered that learning is often deeper and more complex within groups than individually. James Surowiecki's best-selling book *The Wisdom of Crowds*, for example, posits that groups are often smarter than the smartest individuals in them. It is this collective intellectual energy that sparks creative ideas and leads not only to deeper understanding but new learning within a community.

Hephzibah Roskelly in her book *Breaking (into) the Circle: Group Work for Change in the English Classroom* quotes Andrea Lunsford, who researches collaborative writing.

> Lunsford's research led her to make six claims about collaboration that can help teachers think about why group work is crucial to classroom instruction.
>
> 1. Collaboration aids in problem finding as well as problem solving.
> 2. Collaboration aids in learning abstractions.
> 3. Collaboration aids in transfer and assimilation: it fosters interdisciplinary thinking.
> 4. Collaboration leads not only to sharper, more critical thinking, but to a deeper understanding of others.
> 5. Collaboration leads to higher achievement in general.
> 6. Collaboration fosters excellence. (Roskelly 2003, 24–25)

Additionally, as Roskelly points out, "Students learn from peers because they value peers' opinions and are influenced by them in ways they are not influenced by teachers" (32). This is no surprise; as teachers, we know that when we work with others on a project or explore a novel within a book club, our understanding deepens and thoughts expressed by one member will prompt new reflections that we may not have had on our own.

And when *teachers* collaborate, for example, in professional learning communities, student achievement is higher in many content-area subjects. A recent study of students and teachers in a large urban school district found that students showed higher achievement in reading and mathematics when they "attend schools characterized by higher levels of teacher collaboration for school improvement" (Goddard, Goddard, and Tschannen-Moran 2007).

Schools of the future may even look different in order to better accommodate a collaborative environment that encourages interdependence. According to Prakash Nair, founder of an architectural firm specializing in school design, "In the 21st century, education is about project-based learning, independent research, design and creativity, and more than anything else, critical thinking and challenges to old assumptions" (Nair 2009, 24). The firm has built schools throughout the world that have shared community learning centers, open spaces for small-group work, learning studios for direct instruction, reading lofts, and a central atrium for performances. The physical layout of such schools sends a message to students that their learning environment is a microcosm of the world into which they will soon enter. As Nair points out, "Who seriously believes that locking 25 students in a small room with one adult for several hours each day is the best way for them to be 'educated'?" (2009, 1).

Schools don't have to undergo massive renovation, however, to accommodate collaborative learning. Simple changes such as moving desks into pods for group work, allowing partners to sit on the floor for discussions, bringing in furniture that encourages community, or finding unused larger spaces (such as outside courtyards) for performance practice can facilitate systemic change that embraces twenty-first-century learning.

The Value of Discussion

In the traditional classroom, the teacher talks and the students listen, creating a passive learning environment rather than an active one. Similarly, most whole-class discussions are led by teachers and generally engage only one student at a time, while others listen or wait to be called upon. The talk is controlled by a protocol that facilitates order, but "keeping the peace" is not always in the best interest of learning. Such communication can be viewed as straight lines on a plane, from teacher to learner and back to teacher, rather than as intersecting circles that form a multidimensional, inclusive model.

Group work is so important because it helps students develop discussion skills often undervalued in schools, such as the ability to effectively communicate, engage in deliberation, or learn to join individual talents in collective learning. An interactive approach to learning helps learners stay focused and actively engaged as they become immersed in problem solving, critical and creative thinking, and learning within a relevant context. Additionally, as Nel Noddings points out in her work on the ethics of caring, dialogue teaches us to care about each other and thus learn the nuances of interpersonal relationships. Students must learn how to become connected, to really listen to each other, and try to understand others' viewpoints even if they differ radically from their own (Noddings 2005).

Students who may have had less than positive experiences in school or few experiences within a caring community are often the very ones teachers are most reluctant to allow to work collaboratively. Their prior histories may label them as "troublemakers," renegades who lack adequate social skills or don't care enough to contribute to the group's efforts. With such students, however, group learning may be the one vehicle that will keep them in school, especially as they come to realize that their voices are heard and their opinions valued. Once students discover that their contributions are important to others, an upward spiral is created, tapping into students' sense of self-efficacy and intellectual autonomy.

The Habits of Effective Dialogue

The art of dialogue is a process that varies with the topic, the personalities of the participants, and the context, so students must learn to adapt their communication skills to fit the circumstances. Consider helping students begin to think about discussion skills by providing a handout of the habits of effective dialogue found in Figure 4–1 on the next page.

After displaying the list in Figure 4–1, I like to divide the class into small groups based on common interests or friendships so students will feel comfortable discussing these rather open-ended statements. I then assign each group two or more "habits" and ask students to define, in their own words, the meaning of each habit as it might apply to their class, explaining that they are free to disagree with a habit or revise or reword it to better meet their needs. Each group should have:

- a discussion director who facilitates the dialogue
- a recorder to take notes as the group talks
- a reporter, who will share discussion points (report out) with the rest of the class

FIGURE 4–1

Habits of Effective Dialogue (Lent 2006)

- Respect is bedrock.
- Judgment is suspended.
- Listening is paired with empathy and understanding.
- Examination of issues trumps defense of viewpoints.
- Inquiry guides questions and comments.
- Silence is accepted.
- Assumptions are reexamined.
- Spontaneity is encouraged.
- Control is diminished.
- Perspectives are broadened.
- Ambiguity is expected.
- Differences are respected.

Students enjoy this activity and it helps to build community from the outset. They also come up with some great ways to change the wording so it more accurately reflects their language. As one group said about the second habit, "Judgin' ain't cool." When each group has reported out, I ask the class to come up with their own habits of effective dialogue, principles that each person will agree to honor. When we have agreed on our classroom principles, we list them on chart paper and post them in the room as a reminder to all. It is always fascinating to me to see how individual classes come up with slightly different principles, but it is important that each group take ownership for defining the "rules" for its community.

Listening to Each Other

It is often very difficult for multitasking, whirling-dervish teenagers to remain quiet, listen intently, and respond directly to another person's comments. Like all interpersonal skills, this one requires practice. At first, students may need to have pen and paper at hand so they can hold their thoughts by jotting them down while listening. I find this attentive practice grows as students learn how to fit their voices into the pace of discussion. You can help them with this process by placing students with partners and providing passages such as the following, from Jimmy's stories. I give passages to students one at a time and ask them to silently read the passage before beginning the activity.

The hotter the lodge, the more we sang. Some men moaned and grumbled in agony; others writhed, trying to escape the scalding heat. Some wept aloud. Others yelped at the stinging pain. We all were experiencing the fragile flesh wrapped around our bones and heart. How vulnerable; how humbling. (from "The Embrace")

I admit it might have looked like a dumb move on my part if you value only money, as many people do, but sometimes enough stupid moves pile up to make a tidy little karmic stash—and even a few happy days. (from "Saving the Tree")

Say you got to the swing first. You had to pump your legs and thrust your shoulders forward to get as high as you could. There was absolutely no compromise when it came to height, and once you reached the highest point in your swing, you had to bail out. (from "The Swing Test That Made Us Men")

Partner A has the first turn to talk for two minutes, stream-of-consciousness style, about anything the passage brings to mind. Partner B listens without saying a word, although he or she may jot notes if it helps the listener focus. Then, Partner B talks while A listens, making notes if necessary. There may be a follow-up session of two more minutes each, but no interruptions are allowed. I find it helpful to demonstrate this activity with a volunteer before asking students to practice.

This activity can be expanded by having students ask questions of their partner after they listen. The format may look like the following.

- Both partners silently read a passage from a story that has been provided to them by the teacher.
- Partner A responds to the passage for at least two minutes.
- Partner B listens and writes questions that he would like to ask Partner A about his or her response. He or she then asks the questions one at a time, listening for the answer, but not responding. There may be follow-up questions by Partner B if necessary.
- The process is repeated with a different passage. Partner B talks; Partner A asks questions.

After the pairs have had a chance to listen and talk, I ask the class to share their reflections about the activity. Some students may report that they found it difficult to listen without speaking; others may have had trouble talking for two minutes in this staged setting.

As a follow-up, I help students develop "characteristics of a good listener" to post on the classroom wall.

Organizing for Group Work

Although we as teachers may be convinced of the value of group work, we may not always utilize it for a variety of reasons, one of which is the fear that the class may become "out of control," an understandable concern considering the restlessness and energy that many adolescents suppress while sitting quietly listening or writing independently. When we fear a volcanic eruption among students, we may tighten down the valves of control rather than opening a port to allow the pressure to dissipate in a productive way. In any case, I always have to remind myself that group work, like learning itself, rarely clicks into place once and for all. Some days grouping goes beautifully; other days it is an exercise in frustration, for the students as well as for me.

Perhaps one of the most difficult aspects of being a teacher is the struggle for balance, and this is especially true when engaging students in group work. Just know that it will get easier each day until, finally, you will not imagine how you could have taught any other way. Parker Palmer, author of *The Courage to Teach* (1998), offers the following advice on balancing a teaching and learning space. I often find it helpful to return to these tenets when students are actively engaged in working together.

- The space should be bounded and open.
- The space should be hospitable and "charged."
- The space should invite the voice of the individual and the voice of the group.
- The space should honor the "little" stories of the students and the "big" stories of the disciplines and traditions.
- The space should support solitude and surround it with the resources of community.
- The space should welcome both silence and speech. (Palmer 1998, 74)

In addition to balance, I find that structure and organization are essential for successful group learning. There are countless ways of forming groups within a class. One method is simply to have students number off, one through four. All the "ones" will come together, all the "twos," and so forth. For variety, I sometimes place different-colored dots under the tops of the desks and the groups will form according to the color of their dots. This format works best when members of the class have come to know each other well enough to work flexibly with most anyone in the room.

As we discussed in Chapter 2, trust is an important component of group work, so be aware of interpersonal problems. Sometimes issues will work themselves out when kids work together for a common goal, but there is also the possibility that a major eruption will stop the group in its tracks if trust has not been established. In the beginning, I allow students to choose their group members, if possible. Following are other ways of organizing groups.

- *Ability levels*. Group students with similar abilities or try placing those with varying abilities together so they may learn from each other. If you are planning to have students do a reader's theatre based on a story, for example, you may wish to have both strong and weak readers in the group. If you are assigning various poems for groups to read and analyze, you may choose shorter poems for groups of readers who have difficulty reading and longer or more complex poems for those who read well.

- *Interest*. Group students who are interested in the same topic or assignment. For example, some students may be interested in research, others may collaborate on creative writing, and those interested in performance may do a radio theatre (see Chapter 6). Students may also be grouped according to their interest in a theme, such as prejudice, love, or coming of age.

- *Learning styles*. There are many online sites that provide information about learning styles as well as inventories or surveys that will help students determine their modalities. Learning-styles-online.com, for example, provides a nice overview and a quick survey that shows results in a graphic format. Knowing your students' learning styles will allow you to form groups that will help students understand their strengths and learn to improve in areas they may find challenging. For some assignments, I place all auditory students together, perhaps to provide musical accompaniment for a story or poem. Other projects may require a variety of skills, such as having auditory, visual, and kinesthetic learners work together to create a well-rounded product or performance.

Students are often keenly interested in finding out about their own characteristic learning modes. Those students could research Howard Gardner's theory of multiple intelligences. An interactive explanation of Gardner's work can be found on the PBS website, *Beta Thirteen WNET New York* at www.thirteen.org/. Search for "multiple intelligences."

- *Personality traits.* If you place a group of shy students together, you may find that you need to prompt discussion a bit, but such a grouping will encourage quiet students to take part. Extroverted students may vie for the leading role but must learn to share the limelight when they are grouped together. Although it is often helpful to allow students to work with those who are most like themselves, I also find it useful to mix up the group so various strengths are represented.

Group Norms

In Chapter 1, I mention the importance of "inviting students in" by allowing them to make choices about their learning environments. Before beginning group work, I ask students to agree on group norms, sometimes called "ground rules," for their work. First, I brainstorm with the whole class, writing all suggestions on the board, even off-the-wall ones like "everyone must stay awake." Much like the habits for effective dialogue, norms are general statements that target behavior and expectations, such as:

- Everyone will participate in discussions
- Members will signal when they want to interject a comment by _____.
- We will take a time-out if the discussion becomes adversarial or nonproductive.

After brainstorming, I divide the class into groups and ask them to agree on their top five "norms," giving them suggestions for coming to consensus, such as voting, narrowing down the list first, having each member pick their top three choices, and so forth. After each group comes up with their top five, I bring the class back together for a vote. It is sometimes possible to include all of the choices as many of the groups will have chosen the same norms.

Literature Circles

Literature circles have been used by language arts teachers for years as a way to engage students in collaborative learning. According to Daniels and Steineke, who have written extensively about literature circles, the consistent elements of a good literature circle include the following:

- Students choose their own reading materials.
- Small groups (three to six students) are formed, based upon book choice.
- Grouping is by text choices, not by "ability" or other tracking.
- Members write notes that help guide both their reading and their discussion.
- Discussion questions come from the students, not teachers or textbooks.
- Teacher-led minilessons serve as bookends, before and after meetings.
- The teacher does not lead any group, but acts as a facilitator, fellow reader, and observer.
- Personal responses, connections, and questions are the starting point of discussion.
- A spirit of playfulness and sharing pervades the room.
- When books are finished, groups share highlights of their reading with classmates through presentations, reviews, dramatizations, book chats, or other activities.
- Assessment is by teacher observation and student self-evaluation. (Daniels and Steineke 2004, 3–4)

Although a complete exploration of literature circles is beyond the scope of this book, you can go to www.literaturecircles.com for more information on this practice.

Roles

In addition to the guidelines listed above, there is an aspect of literature circle work that may be helpful as you guide students through Jimmy's stories. Many teachers begin literature circles by assigning, or allowing students to choose, roles for group work. Daniels and Steineke offer a note of caution about roles, however, saying that they may "evoke mechanical, pro forma discussions rather than sparkling conversation" (2004, 76). I have experienced this downside to using roles in my own work with literature circles, especially if the task related to the role is too narrowly defined or students have yet to discover the spontaneous and fulfilling flow of a deep discussion. Often, when students complete the task for their roles, they report that they are "finished," and the dialogue ends, so I do advocate monitoring carefully how students are using roles. As a way to initiate group work, however, roles can provide students with a safe place from which to venture into meaningful discussion.

Discuss with students the various roles that they may take in a group. Following are names and descriptions of roles that appeal to students.

- *Discussion director.* This role is one of facilitator whose primary task is to move the conversation deeper by prompting everyone to respond or by asking follow-up questions, rephrasing comments so they are clearly understood, or encouraging each person to contribute. He will also connect the discussion to the text, finding and presenting passages to the group that may elicit dialogue. An explicit caution is sometimes necessary: This role does not grant the director permission to dominate or "boss around" other members of the group.

- *Recorder.* This member takes notes of the discussion, perhaps on a computer, while at the same time participating in the discussion. The highlights of the discussion should be made available to all group members and may be shared with the entire class or used to create a project or performance.

- *Illuminator.* This person identifies and "illuminates" passages that are particularly well written, thought provoking, difficult to understand, or deserving of attention. She will read each identified passage, note briefly why it is illuminated, and ask for others' comments. The purpose of this role is to encourage students to learn to read carefully and pay attention to nuances of the text.

- *Vocabulary finder*. This "word" person will target words in the text that others may not understand or words that are used in unusual ways. He finds the meanings of the words by asking the teacher or others about them, looking them up (but *not* providing a simple dictionary definition) or just bringing them up for discussion with the group.

- *Connector*. This role is for the person who can find connections between passages in the text and other texts, media, or online sources. She may also help members of the group respond to passages by asking if anyone found a personal connection to something in the text.

- *Researcher*. This role often falls to the techie. He finds something within the text that the group may want to know more about: a person or place mentioned in the text, a time period, or something about the author. The researcher often uses online sources to expand group learning.

- *Summarizer/reader*. Although this role may seem simplistic, it is often challenging because it requires that the person understand what is important to recount from the story. This same person may be asked to read a story to the group with expression as others read silently.

As you can see, there is no end to the roles that can be utilized depending upon the text and the purpose for reading. When I ask students what roles they may want, I am often surprised by what they come up with: illustrator, poetry finder, social director, time manager, encourager, musical, social, or performance director.

Daniels and Steineke suggest a multipurpose role sheet where all students address components of the story in writing before coming together to discuss. Such a role sheet might ask students to mark any passages that "stick out" for them, note any reactions or connections they may have to the text, jot down anything they notice about the author's craft, or write any questions that came to mind while reading (2007, 77). You, as the teacher, can also customize role sheets according to your students' needs.

Using Roles with Jimmy's Works

How might a literature circle look after students read Jimmy's "Wells Market"?

- The summarizer would go first, recounting the events of the story. You may want to make sure the summarizer in each group understands that Jimmy includes a flashback in this story, as this may confuse some readers.

- Next, the vocabulary finder would point out and explain vocabulary such as *mythic proportions*, *bunting*, *sorority*, *aghast*, *rectory*, *chalice*, *resilient*, *gurney*, or, best of all, *pontifical decorum*. You should not create a list of words for this role, nor should you intervene unless the group is missing a word that is essential to the understanding of the story. It is important for students to learn which words they need to define for deeper comprehension. The vocabulary finder may also ask others in the group to contribute words as they read.

- The illuminator may point out passages such as "folded in on itself like a butterfly's time to die in winter, curled up to endure its own solitude" as an example of beautiful (or figurative) language or "I-want-to-see-my-grandma . . . and-you-can-have-the-gloves" for the unusual way it is written to emphasize the difficulty of Jimmy's decision.

- The researcher has much to choose from in this story. He may want to find out about Sonny Liston and provide a picture of him or a history of his championship. Ben Hur is mentioned twice in the story, so the researcher may bring in a snippet of the old movie for his group to watch to give students a sense of Jimmy's role model when he was young.

- The connector could facilitate a nice discussion by reading the sentence "I would willingly, evenly gratefully, accept the sorrow of life if I'd just be allowed to see my grandma once a year during Christmas" and asking the group about their relationship with their grandparents. She could also ask if anyone had ever seen one of the movies Jimmy mentioned in the story.

- Finally, the group is ready for a deeper discussion of the story, with the discussion director facilitating. He would refer directly to the text as a jumping-off point for discussion, perhaps with the teacher's help at first.
  - Jimmy admitted that he stole from the sorority girls so he would have gifts to give his mother in case she came to visit. How should the nuns have balanced this theft with Jimmy's motive? Is stealing ever justified?

- What do you think of Johnny La'O? Have you ever known guys like him? Do you think he really cared about Jimmy or was he just using him?
- Jimmy's grandmother didn't recognize him and actually hit him with her cane. Have any of you had an experience you would be willing to share about a relative who has Alzheimer's?

You could scaffold this practice by providing a short text and having all students in the class go through each of the roles, one at a time, so they understand how the process works. The ultimate goal, of course, is that students will not need roles, that they will fall naturally into a lively discussion, and all of the tasks assigned in roles will emerge during the course of conversation. But be patient. As we know through our own collegial conversations sometimes discussions are exciting and thought-provoking . . . and sometimes they simply aren't.

What we can count on is that with each group experience, students will take incremental steps toward becoming not only independent but *inter*dependent, learning to rely on each other as they take a journey together. It's the process, the inherent give-and-take, and the experience of interaction that will move students into a new realm of learning, one that will stay with them long after they have read the last page of the text.

Further Reading

Breaking (into) the Circle: Group Work for Change in the English Classroom (Roskelly 2003)

Mini-Lessons for Literature Circles (Daniels and Steineke 2004)

Speaking Volumes: How to Get Students Discussing Books—and Much More (Gilmore 2006)

5 Writing and Learning

People ask, "How do you write so much," or "What do you write about?" and I answer that there is no easy way, no magic or gift or genius or talent, just the deep desire in my soul to find words. . . .

—Jimmy Santiago Baca

Jimmy and I were surprised and pleased when so many young people showed up voluntarily for a writing workshop—on a Saturday afternoon. After the teenagers were seated in a wide circle, Jimmy began by telling a personal story as a way to introduce himself, to connect with the students, and get them thinking.

He then illuminated the point of the story, "We should never allow others to take away our gifts, our inner beauty, the part of ourselves that shines through no matter how others try to douse our light."

That led to my writing prompt: "Write about who you are, not the person others think you are, not who you may pretend to be, but about the core you, that solid, unique personality that dwells within each of us."

We urged the students to freewrite and to keep writing, even when they felt they had nothing left to say. As always, the room became quiet as writers engaged in the often uneasy experience of discovering that the pen can be the diviner of the soul. Soon, the writing momentum increased as self-reflection gave way to greater understanding.

On another Saturday in another workshop, Jimmy told students about his mother's choice not to return to her children when a tractor-trailer failed to pick her up as she was hitchhiking back home. That instantaneous decision dramatically changed her life as well as the lives of Jimmy and his siblings, as you will hear when you watch Jimmy tell this story on the DVD found in the front of this book. (See "Tractor-Trailer Moment" on the video's menu.)

Students then wrote about their own "tractor-trailer" moments, events in their lives that changed them forever. After writing for almost twenty minutes, one student offered to read her piece aloud, and it became one of those memorable spaces in time—that flash of understanding when one person sees through the eyes of another, where empathy is whetted, awareness of others is born, human connections are sealed. She described her father's death when she was very young and how the event tilted her universe irrevocably. Other students wiped tears from their eyes as they listened. Thus, writing on that day had invisibly moved from the inner to the outer, leaving a thread of awareness.

Writing has the power not only to transform individuals but to knit together communities by evoking trust, common experience, and compassion. In *The Writing Life*, Annie Dillard quotes Graham Greene who once said that it may take many years to write a novel, but "The author is not the same man at the end of the book as he was at the beginning" (Dillard 1990, 14). The same can be said for students who are allowed to write regularly in a classroom. As they become writers, they change through an act that we can neither force nor coerce: reflection.

Why Write?

What is becoming increasingly clear through research is that writing promotes critical thinking, which, in turn, leads directly to increased learning. The National Writing Project makes clear this connection. "Writing is a complex activity; more than just a skill or talent, it is a means of inquiry and expression for learning in all grades and disciplines" (2006, 3). The advantages of writing are also well documented.

> Research found that writing could develop higher-order thinking skills: analyzing, synthesizing, evaluating, and interpreting. The very difficulty of writing is its virtue: it requires that students move beyond rote learning and simply reproducing information, facts, dates, and formulae. Students must also learn how to question their own

assumptions and reflect critically on an alternative or opposing view-point. (National Writing Project 2006, 23)

Perhaps the National Commission on Writing put it best when they wrote in their report, *The Neglected "R"*: "Writing is not simply a way for students to demonstrate what they know. It is a way to help them understand what they know. At its best, writing is learning" (The National Commission on Writing 2003, 13).

What *Is* Writing?

The concept of writing has drastically changed from the 1970s until today. From the nineteenth century until the 1970s, writing was seen as a means of "learning and assessing a sequence of essential skills; forming letters, building vocabulary, identifying parts of speech, diagramming sentences, mastering grammar and punctuation, and following paragraph types and genres of writing according to prescribed conventions" (National Writing Project 2006, 19). This emphasis on mechanical errors "overshadowed the deep, rhetorical, social, and cognitive possibilities of writing for communication and critical thinking" (National Writing Project 2006, 20).

Even today, that sense of "correctness" often undermines the process of writing—that is, the process of thinking. Fortunately, we now understand that teaching grammar in isolation does not transfer to student writing (Hillocks 1986) and that this part of the writing process is best addressed during the editing stage. Indeed, with spell check, the need for the lethal red pen is becoming obsolete.

As for writing itself, good teachers know that writing is not linear—any-thing but—and a perfectly "correct" piece may lack conviction, creativity, or what I call "oomph." The process itself is often messy, a cognitively challenging puzzle that fits together one day and refuses to snap into place the next. But it is through the *process* of writing that students are able to engage in deep and complex thinking that underlies unforgettable pieces.

Many students say they don't like to write, perhaps because they may never have experienced the flow that comes from getting lost in writing, the tension inherent in the exploration of ideas, or the exhilaration of their own magic rising up from the pages. "School" writing is often so far removed from real writing that they seem to have little in common. Students have learned to answer questions by packing in words to earn a higher grade, write contrived, formulaic five-paragraph essays on every topic thrown at them, and like boxers in a ring, fight against the clock while composing timed pieces for standardized tests where stakes are high and the possibility of a total knockout is frighteningly real.

How can we help students become better writers for school and life, while showing them how to fill their papers with "the breathings of the heart" as William Wordsworth once said? The best we can do as their coaches is to immerse them in a process that generally works, help them feel safe enough to use it, guide them in their endeavors, and then enthusiastically celebrate their success.

A Writing Process

Much research supports the concept of writing as a recursive activity, with writers moving into and out of various phases of composition. For example, when students read Jimmy's "Saving the Tree" (page 138) and write about something *they* tried to save, they may plan what they want to write, draft their piece, return to planning as they consider reorganization, revise the introduction, and so on. While writing does not follow a prescribed process, good writers generally use some variation of the following to produce their best pieces:

- planning (generating ideas, setting goals, and organizing)
- translating (turning plans into written language)
- reviewing (evaluating and revising) (National Writing Project 2006, 25)

Teachers can help students understand and utilize this process by allowing them to experience each phase and by constantly demonstrating through mentor texts, such as Jimmy's stories or poems, how "real" writers use language to communicate ideas.

Prewriting

All writers need time to think, to get their brain juices flowing, sometimes even before putting pen to paper or finger to key. That's why prompts are so invaluable. When students read about Jimmy's yearning to see his grand-mother in the story "Wells Market" (see page 92), for example, they begin to think of times when they missed someone they loved and the impetus to create their own personal history begins to take hold. Additionally, as they study Jimmy's style, they come to see how he crafts the piece through flash-back, dialogue, and humor—elements they can utilize when they begin their own drafts.

With the explosion of "programs" for writing, usually costing thou-sands of dollars, many teachers come to believe every student must "prewrite" by using a graphic organizer or other clever strategy to stimu-late ideas. What we really want, however, is for students to learn to gener-ate ideas in the way that works best for them, such as brainstorming, freewriting, drawing, discussing, mapping, listing, or outlining. I make a jot list first to get my thoughts organized; Jimmy, on the other hand, sits down and the words seem to run straight from his head down his arms and through his fingers, his best lines often conceived in the moment. My first draft is organized chaos; Jimmy's more randomly creative. We will never turn kids into writers by mandating how they should write. What we can offer students is time—to think, to plan, and to read voraciously.

Drafting

During the drafting stage, a writer forms her ideas into a coherent, satisfy-ing whole, depending upon the purpose, audience, and complexity of the writing task. Here, writers experiment with elements such as voice, word choice, or organization, letting all thoughts emerge before taming them into a final copy. Much like riders learning to control a bicycle so it will become a vehicle to take them where they want to go, writers must balance a com-position's many elements so that it serves their own purposes.

Revising

Revision is perhaps the most difficult aspect of writing for both students and teachers because it is such an individualized process, one that students are often reluctant to attempt. Teens are impatient by nature and addicted to instant gratification, so they want to see their initial pieces as finished, often stating emphatically they have nothing else to add or change. Although it may be true that once in a while someone writes something that is "perfect" the first time around, for the vast majority of writers, revision is simply a part of the process. Students must be shown *how* to revise, however, instead of merely being told *to* revise. Once they get it, they will understand what Robert Cormier, beloved young adult author, meant when he said, "The beautiful part of writing is that you don't have to get it right the first time, unlike, say, a brain surgeon. You can always do it better, find the exact word, the apt phrase, the leaping simile."

How to Revise

One of the best ways to help students learn to revise is to show them your writer's underbelly. Put a piece of your writing out there, swallow hard, and ask them how you could make it better. Once students see that you are willing to be vulnerable and take the risk you are asking of them, they will rise to the occasion—and they will begin to see how revision can vastly improve any piece of writing. If you aren't sure about the process of revision yourself, one simple question will usually do the trick: "What more do you want to know?"

Kelly Gallagher, author of *Teaching Adolescent Writers* (2006), conducts a "question flood" in his class where he shows students a short draft that he intentionally has underwritten. Students then produce a flood of questions, many beginning with age-old question words such as, "Why, when, how much, where, what."

Barry Gilmore, author and teacher, provides revision suggestions for his students, such as the following:

- Consider multiple approaches to organizing your information.
- Go back to the evidence.
- Go with your instincts.
- Explain your organization out loud to someone else.
- Check your transitions.
- Check the end of paragraphs. Be certain they tie back to the ideas you've already presented.
- Make lists. Try listing details or ideas in columns and see if they square up the way you think they do.
- Think of your essay as a map. Where does it start? Where does it end? Does it go somewhere or just go in circles? (Gilmore 2007, 34)

Peer Revision

We all need a trusted peer who will tell us the truth about our writing and, at the same time, encourage us in our endeavors. In the classroom, that trusted peer is called a *writing partner*. Such partners come to know each other's style and learn how to become invaluable writing coaches if the match is a good one. Although several of the following activities include suggested prompts for revision, the goal is for students to become experienced and comfortable enough with the writing process that eventually they will have no need of prompts. As they become better writers themselves, they will also gain the skills to help their partners improve their pieces. Figure 5–1 shows how partners can work together to help each other revise.

Group Revision

Group revision is another effective way to get students thinking about how they could improve their papers. In addition, teachers have found that when students know others will be reading what they have written, they take their writing more seriously. See Figure 5–2 for a group-revision activity.

FIGURE 5–1

Peer Revision

Partner A will listen *intently* as the paper is read by Partner B or will read the paper silently. She will then answer two or more of the following questions orally or by writing in the margins of the rough draft. Partner B will then do the same for Partner A's paper.

1. What is the best part of the piece? Why?
2. What more do you want to know?
3. Does the writer include "rabbit trails" that take you away from his or her central message or story? If so, point them out.
4. How could your partner improve the beginning?
5. Does the conclusion "wrap up" the piece? If not, how could it be improved?
6. Find at least five words, phrases, or sentences that the writer could replace to make the piece more lively or clear.
7. Anything else?

Note to the writer: You do not have to take all or any of the suggestions made by your partner. Think about what she says and conference with another person or your teacher if you aren't sure about how to revise your paper.

FIGURE 5-2

Group Revision Activity

Instructions

1. Decide who will go first. That person will read her paper aloud to the group.
2. Every other member of the group will listen carefully and take notes as the paper is being read. It is often helpful to have each listener pay attention to only one aspect of the paper, as suggested by the focus questions for listeners below.
3. When the writer finishes reading, each writer will say what he likes best about the paper.
4. Members will each use their notes to make one recommendation to the writer.
5. All the notes go to the writer to help with revision.

Focus Questions for Listeners

1. What do you want to know more about?
2. Does the introduction catch your attention? If not, how could it be improved?
3. Does the conclusion do its job? If not, do you have any suggestions?
4. What did the writer leave out? Should it be included?
5. What did the writer include that is distracting and could be left out?
6. What type of organization does the writer use? Does it work?
7. Are the verbs active? Are there any verbs that could be replaced?
8. Which of the adjectives would you change if you were the writer? Would you leave any out?
9. Where can the writer stretch out the moment?
10. Overall, what can you say to help the writer improve the piece?

Editing

It is only after students have finished revising the content of their piece of writing that they concentrate on the conventions of their writing. Now is the time to pay close attention to spelling, punctuation, and grammar. Remember, however, that even the most talented writer may not be a talented speller, that no one is immune to a comma error, and that copy editors would not have jobs if everyone were grammarians. Allow students to become specialists during the editing process. One student (or team) may have the comma rules down while another is a great speller and a third can remember how to punctuate dialogue. Students can consult each other as they strive to make their writing as correct as possible.

Teacher Feedback

How many students really read those comments teachers spend hours writing in the margins of graded papers? The time to coach students is *during* the writing process, not after the game is over. When teachers act as a knowledgeable partner *while* students are writing, they are able to nudge them toward shifts in understanding that will be reflected in their final papers. Practice using the questions in Figure 5–3 to help students reflect on their own writing during the drafting and revision process. The key is simply responding to students human to human, not teacher to student, often during short, individual conferences with students.

A Word About Assessment

Give yourselves and your students a break and resist the urge to grade every piece of writing students produce. If writing is purposeful, the audience is authentic, and the writer has gained self-efficacy, grading papers will be of secondary concern. Give students every opportunity to produce their best piece of writing to be turned in for a grade by having them keep a portfolio of their writing. Some pieces may be works in progress, some may be personal pieces students never intend to have you grade, and others may be almost complete. The portfolio may contain essays, research papers, letters, poetry, fiction, or reflective writing, for example. Students will choose a

---

FIGURE 5–3

Teacher Feedback Prompts

1. Why did you choose to . . . ?
2. How might your thinking have changed if you had . . . ?
3. I was wondering . . . ?
4. Have you considered . . . ?
5. I have a question about this.
6. I'm not sure I understand . . .
7. This part of the piece is brilliant! Toward the end, however, you seem to lose your momentum. Can you figure out why?
8. I want to know more. What happened then?
9. How would your piece change if you moved this part here?
10. You seem to be holding back. I just don't hear your voice in this piece. Why don't you try freewriting for a while?

---

piece to finish for a grade every couple of weeks, but they will write or revise each day. At the end of the year, portfolios should be returned to the student.

What to Write

Once teachers begin to think of writing as a means of fostering inquiry, problem solving, reflection, clarification, and discovery, they see daily opportunities for its use instead of relegating writing to an occasional essay or an answer to a question on a test. Even when teachers are convinced that students should be writing regularly and in a variety of ways, however, they still may not be sure *what* students should be writing. Additionally, some teachers don't see themselves as writers, perhaps feeling insecure about providing suggestions to student-writers and thus about incorporating writing into their curriculum. So, how can writing be used in classrooms on a daily basis, and how can teachers learn to help students become better writers?

First of all, students learn to write by writing (National Council of Teachers of English 1985). It follows that any curriculum time devoted to writing is beneficial not only in increasing students' writing skills but also in helping them understand content. Writing, like reading, is a tool for learning and should be a part of every class every day. Following are practices that support writing in any content area.

Learning Logs

A learning log is used by students as a way of deepening or reinforcing learning. Science learning logs are especially helpful as students record notes during experiments, describe procedures, or explain concepts or processes in their own words, such as how a cell divides or the theory of natural selection. Social studies teachers use learning logs as places where students can deconstruct historical events, note questions they may have, or write how they feel about occurrences in history they may find disturbing or confusing. In English class, students may use their learning logs to record punctuation rules they have trouble remembering, for instance, or ways to combine sentences so that their writing is more interesting. They may also use their logs to write personal responses to fiction or poetry.

It is a good idea for students to devote a page or two of their notebooks to their own spelling demons or new vocabulary words they encounter while reading. Give students plenty of time to use their logs in class before, during, or after instruction. Note that learning logs are often checked by the teacher only for completion.

Writer's Notebook

Writer's notebooks are student-selected, not school-issued, and are used by students to develop their "writer's eye." Students may use their notebooks to record events, experiences, people, or places; many students also use these writing tools to make lists, perhaps of favorite music or books. Encourage students to personalize their notebooks by copying lyrics, poems, or favorite passages—or even composing their own poems, song lyrics, or short stories. Make sure notebooks contain pockets of some sort because often students want to place tangible pieces of their lives in their notebooks, such as tickets to a concert, photographs, or notes from friends, all of which may be later used as prompts for writing. This notebook will become an invaluable tool for planting the seeds of future writing pieces, and many students keep these notebooks forever. Generally, the writer's notebook is not graded.

Journals

This type of notebook is not a diary, despite its name. Although students often write pieces of a personal nature in their journals, its primary purpose is to hold classroom writings, generally in response to a prompt at the beginning of class. Sometimes, teachers will provide a prompt related to the topic of study: a quote, problem, question, or thought-provoking fact or idea. Students then are allowed five to ten minutes to write. This is a whole-class activity, not one that students do in their free time, and the class is quiet as students write. Students develop writing fluency through this activity as they practice various types of writing. Teachers often walk around the room, making sure everyone is writing, giving checks for participation. You may also require that students choose a piece every so often to turn in or revise into a final copy for a grade. If time allows, discussions that follow journal writing can turn into engaging "teachable moments" where new concepts are introduced and old ones reinforced. This is also a great "bellringer" activity that allows students time to settle in before instruction begins.

Journal Prompts

Journal writing works especially well when students themselves provide the prompt in the form of an open-ended question. You could assign each student a day to be responsible for sharing a suitable prompt. Kids will often scour the newspaper, magazines, online articles, short stories, or poetry to come up with an unusual or thought-provoking prompt for their classmates to write about. You might decide to limit the prompts to certain topics so the writing correlates to your content. It also may be helpful to have students practice creating prompts so they understand that a good prompt requires deeper thinking than a low-level, easy-to-answer prompt.

Journal Prompts from Jimmy's Stories

Students could practice writing prompts after reading one of Jimmy's poems or stories. For example, in the story "Didn't Mean To" (in the student book, *Stories from the Edge*), Jimmy touches on several themes that students could examine in more depth. The following examples show how students could pull passages from the stories to create a prompt that will most likely produce thoughtful writing.

- Jimmy writes, "The group in the room was divided into races—Chicanos/Mexicans and Native Americans on one side; Crips and Bloods in another corner; Asian and Whites in the middle but separate. The kids had that look in their eyes, that glare of hurt mixed with rage and defiance. What had happened during these nine months to raise the scale of hatred between races so high?"
  - Prompt: Why do you think the "scale of hatred" between races is often so high?
- Jimmy said that people who are in jail have to wear "unmoving masks" to protect themselves.
  - Prompt: What masks do the people at your school wear? Why?
- Jimmy suggests that sometimes young men commit crimes to gain respect or to find their "manhood."

- Prompt: Do you agree? In your opinion, why do young men (or women) commit crimes?

Digital Writing

Students live in a world of digital communication, so this mode of writing is almost always met with enthusiasm. What's more, there is virtually no end to the types of quick assignments, in-depth projects, or collaborative writing that digital tools, such as blogs, wikis, and Facebook, offer. As an example, groups of students could set up nings to facilitate discussion about one of Jimmy's stories. Check out www.pbworks.com/academic/wiki, an online service that hosts safe classroom workspaces.

Open the discussions to the entire school or community as students will profit from examining Jimmy's stories through the experiences of others. This mode of writing may well be a vehicle for bringing together disparate groups as the dialogue takes on a life of its own and kids begin to respond to each other in authentic, relevant ways. Other projects that tap into the community are discussed in Chapter 6.

Hearing Our Students

Jimmy shared with me a draft of a story about doing a workshop at a steel mill town in Indiana. The workers and their families were despondent, "locked away in this huge monstrous city of steel, closed-down lives, hulking lives, padlocked and ominous lives that would express their despair in addiction and violence" (Baca n.d.).

Jimmy gave the steelworkers an assignment: "Imagine that you only have tonight to share with the world who you are. Imagine that tomorrow you'll be gone and now is your opportunity to tell the world you passed this way; you have a name, dreams, a history, and a private life of the heart and mind. Write a letter informing the world that you will not go from this place unknown, that this letter will make you a known person, someone special for the many reasons you will now write."

Jimmy later said, "They wanted to be heard."

Our students, too, want to be heard. And it is through writing that they often discover their strongest, truest voices.

Further Reading

Because Writing Matters: Improving Student Writing in Our Schools
(National Writing Project and Nagin 2006)
Is It Done Yet? Teaching Adolescents the Art of Revision (Gilmore 2007)
Teaching Writing That Matters: Tools and Projects That Motivate Adolescent Writers (Gallagher and Lee 2008)

6 Performances and Projects

I appear here before you all, with a heart.
—Jimmy Santiago Baca, "Jewelry Store"

Kids are natural actors. If you don't believe that even the shyest students can turn into hams and show-offs, just give them a part in a reader's theatre and leave the room for a few minutes. Teachers have the power to resurrect the last vestiges of childhood in their adolescent students when they allow them opportunities to perform. Those days of playing dress up or using stick swords to fight fire-breathing dragons seem suddenly closer when older kids are simply allowed to be kids.

On the enclosed DVD, you will see Jimmy telling students a story, "Man on the Beach," about a time when he learned that he was still capable of negatively judging and stereotyping other people. The story involves an old man following Jimmy and his family while they were walking along the beach in San Diego.

After the students heard the whole story from Jimmy's point of view, students were asked to imagine that they were the old man and to write down what *he* might have been thinking while he walked with his dog near Jimmy's family.

Next, students wrote down what they might have said to Jimmy if they were that man. Then they took turns standing in front of the class playing the roles of Jimmy and "the man on the beach" using intonation, gestures, and facial expressions to enhance the meaning of the words they had written. The rest of us were the perfect audience, "ahhhing" at a great phrase, laughing at a funny line, hooting when the "man" taught Jimmy a lesson in acceptance. Not only were students learning about how literacy is used, but they were building community at the same time.

Performance

Although performances are enjoyable for kids, this instructional practice has pedagogical value as well. Jeffrey Wilhelm in *"You Gotta BE the Book"* (2008) cites research showing that less proficient readers view reading as a decoding process rather than as active meaning making. In an effort to support reading as a dynamic construction of meaning, he looked to drama to create a context for more "sophisticated comprehension and the creation of elaborated meanings" (2008, 124). As such, Wilhelm created what he referred to as "story drama," where students enter a character's point of view or attitude and enact a situation of conflict (133).

Students reported that "making choices" and "doing things," as opposed to simply reading the text, helped them not only overcome their decoding problems but also enjoy the experience of literature while rethinking the act of reading and their roles as readers (146). Additionally, Wilhelm noted, "Drama is an invaluable way to assist kids to use critical literacy as they engage in critical inquiry and understanding" (152). English language learners can also profit from the oral aspects of using language in such a nonthreatening, engaging way.

Interacting with Text

Jimmy's stories are rife with opportunities for first-class performances. We have seen students quickly learn how to use characters, dialogue, or scenes from the stories as jumping-off points for a bit of improvisation.

In the story "Saving the Tree" (page 138), for example, Jimmy writes that he asked a woman if he could buy an old house she had for sale because he wanted to save a tree on the property that she intended to cut down. "I told her I had a little money, not much, and I was anxious to ask her the price. When she said $90,000, I had to breathe in with effort to keep my composure. It was way more than I could afford. My only hope was to come back and see her and beg her to lower the price."

After reading, ask students to write what words Jimmy might use to convince the woman to lower the price. After a student reads his or her piece (or improvs), ask someone else to respond from the woman's point of view. Students could also perform a monologue of what Jimmy might say to the tree before and after he bought the property.

Each of Jimmy's stories has scenes where students could become more deeply involved with the text through acting, and several of the accompanying lessons offer suggestions for having students read the stories creatively. After students have written and performed a few, they will be able to find their own "play" within the stories. Remind them that they are actually writing mini-screenplays and, as the writers, they can use their imaginations to create anything they like.

Freeze Frame

Freeze frame is a dramatic technique in which actors freeze at a particular moment in a play to enhance the climax of the story or an important scene. One character then talks to the audience, revealing his personal thoughts about the situation. In "Magic Marble" (page 88), for example, students could have fun acting out the scene where Cavalo chases Jimmy when he discovers he has stolen his glass eye. Actors would "freeze" and reveal what Cavalo is thinking. The student who is acting as Jimmy could also "freeze" and reveal his thoughts.

Wilhelm expands this activity with what he calls "Snapshot and Tableaux Dramas," where students freeze while acting out part of a story and then "physically or artistically depict the 'freezing' of particular scenes as moments in time that show physical or emotional relationships, and display character gestures, expressions, and activities" (Wilhelm 2008, 134). Sometimes he also asks students to draw a series of such snapshots, "a visual depiction of a story sequence through the use of several pictures and accompanying captions or scripts" and then explain how and why they created it (2008, 134).

Reader's Theatre

A reader's theatre is exactly what the term implies—a performance where actors read from the text and use their voices to convey meaning, usually without costumes, props, or staging. This activity is important because it can improve students' fluency while at the same time foster a deeper understanding of the text as they interpret it through voice, gestures, and body language. Perhaps most importantly, students learn to work with each other to create a performance that other students will enjoy.

Creating Reader's Theatre from Stories

In the story "Repo Man" (found in *Stories from the Edge*, the student edition), Jimmy describes how he desperately tried to keep his car from being repossessed. Starting with the line "It was not long before I bought my own car and it was a doozy," students can create a compelling reader's theatre performance. Here's how it could look:

STUDENT ONE: This would be the narrator, reading from Jimmy's perspective the background leading up to the attempted repossession. Soon, he misses a payment and the collection agency calls begin.

STUDENT TWO: This student can be Jimmy talking to the callers. In some places, he doesn't tell the reader exactly what the caller said, but here is an opportunity for students to create the dialogue based on Jimmy's description and incorporate it into the reader's theatre.

STUDENT THREE: When we are introduced to another caller, this time a man, it gives another student an opportunity to play a "part."

STUDENT FOUR: Finally, there's Pitbull Repo, and it doesn't take much imagination to think what *her* voice sounds like (with a recording of a dog barking in the background when she speaks).

"Eleven Cents" (page 103) is a great story for the entire class to use as practice because it is full of tension and dialogue. Divide kids into groups of five, four characters (including Jimmy) and a narrator. Allow them to perform the story for another group or the entire class. At the end of each performance, have them note how intonation, volume, and tone can create different interpretations of the same words. You get the idea—and so will your students as they read, interpret, interact with each other, and find joy in text. (See Figure 6–1 for guidelines for reader's theatre.)

FIGURE 6–1

Guidelines for Reader's Theatre

1. Give students a story to work with or allow them to choose a story they want to use for their reader's theatre.
2. The number of students needed for each reader's theatre will be determined by the text.
3. Students will reread the story together, perhaps with one person reading orally and the others following along silently, making notes.
4. Students will discuss who will read what parts and determine which scene or descriptions are straight dialogue or which ones could be turned into dialogue (with students taking small liberties by filling in words the character might have said based on Jimmy's descriptions). Note that reader's theatre is not the place for taking substantial creative liberties as they might with other activities.
5. Every group will need a narrator to read the background text.
6. Traditional props aren't necessary, but students often enjoy finding music to accompany the performance or donning simple costumes such as hats or gloves. Students may opt to dress similarly for effect, say in all black.
7. Give students enough time to practice so their performance is relatively glitch-free.
8. Consider allowing groups to perform for other classes or create an afternoon performance for parents or the community.

Radio Theatre

An adaptation of reader's theatre is radio theatre, where students read a story without being seen. They may stand behind an improvised screen for the performance—or record their voices and play the broadcast for their audience. Since gestures and facial expression aren't part of radio theatre, students must rely on their voices to express meaning. They may wish to incorporate sound effects to jazz up the performance.

Overheard

In this performance, students create a scene based on the events in one of Jimmy's stories by allowing the class to overhear a conversation related to the story. In response to "The Warden" (page 132), for example, the class would "overhear" the warden telling his wife about his evening: how the guest of honor was a prisoner he had once guarded, how he felt when he recognized Jimmy, why he left the room. After viewing Jimmy tell the story "Tractor-Trailer Moment" on the accompanying DVD, students could imagine overhearing Jimmy's mother explaining to a waitress at an all-night coffee shop why she came into the diner instead of continuing to try to find a ride to take her back to her children. Groups of students can work together to write the dialogue that is "overheard" and perform it for the other groups. It is fascinating to hear students' different interpretations of the characters for whom they write dialogue.

Directing the Show

This activity involves having students plan the movie version of a story. Here they will make decisions such as where the movie will be shot, which famous actors might play certain parts, how sensitive scenes will be filmed, what music will be used, and which parts of the movie will be used in previews. Students will explain their plan to their classmates, who will then act as famous directors interested in filming the project. Students may then produce a book trailer of their story. More information about this engaging activity can be found on www.squidoo.com/booktrailers, which utilizes programs on computers to create what is similar to a "movie trailer" for the story.

This is a good opportunity for students with various "intelligences" or learning styles to shine by creating posters for the movie, bringing in music that could be used in the soundtrack, or demonstrating their talent with technology, for example.

Poetry Coffee House

Several of the lessons accompanying the stories offer suggestions for having students translate their writing into poems. Additionally, students who come to love Jimmy's stories may wish to read his poems, available online and in several volumes of poetry.

To help students appreciate the oral tradition of poetry, a coffee house event creates an unforgettable experience. Every student will participate in reading one or more original poems that they have spent extensive class time writing and revising. If students have difficulty composing poems, they may model their own poem after one of Jimmy's or another poet's.

Allow students to plan the event by having them sign up for "coffee house committees" such as the following:

- *Publicity*. This committee makes invitations for their friends, parents, teachers, and others whom the class decides to invite.

- *Decorating*. This committee will find a place (perhaps an outdoor restaurant, a section of the school cafeteria, or even the classroom) and will be in charge of transforming the space into a coffee house.

- *Logistics*. This organization committee will make sure everything is in place: a microphone if possible, comfortable chairs for the audience, a stool for the performing poet, programs, and coffee or hot chocolate.

In the News

In this "performance," students will act as television or Web reporters covering news that may emerge from Jimmy's stories. One student will take the part of the reporter, another student will be an eyewitness, and others will take roles as needed, based on the story. For example, in the story "Wells Market" (page 92), Sonny Liston gives Jimmy a pair of his boxing gloves. Students may report the event by interviewing the young Jimmy, a head nun at the orphanage, or any of the kids who lived with Jimmy. A student could also read Liston's fascinating biography online and then pretend to be the boxer as he answers questions from a reporter. As an added bonus, have students "broadcast" a short clip about Sonny Liston to give the audience background information.

Projects

Project work offers students opportunities to learn through activities that foster teamwork, critical thinking, and application of new knowledge. The Partnership for 21st Century Skills (www.21stcenturyskills.org) notes that students need the following skills to become successful in this century.

- creativity and innovation
- critical thinking and problem solving
- communication and collaboration

The development of such skills is a natural part of project-based learning.

Eric Jensen, a leading expert on brain research, also supports the notion that learning involves more than attaining basic skills or memorizing isolated facts. He notes,

> [D]ata suggests that schools would do well to focus on much more real-world learning. Field trips, simulations, role plays, apprenticeships, community service work, and away from school activities that use school knowledge and skills make much more sense than a focus on field-independent classroom learning. The bottom line is that what people know is very highly embedded in the context of the task they're doing. (2006, 21–22)

Just as with adults, when students do something that has a real purpose, they begin to internalize ideas that may have been abstract notions in the printed text.

Projects That Support Social Justice

Jimmy's stories are about social injustices, human frailties, and life unvarnished. Through these stories, students gain awareness of social issues and, as they engage in projects that address such issues, they often feel the stirrings of empowerment and self-efficacy.

The National Research Council in its groundbreaking book, *How People Learn: Brain, Mind, Experience, and School* (2000), addresses the importance of altruism in making learning relevant. "Learners of all ages are more motivated when they can see the usefulness of what they are learning and when they can use that information to do something that has an impact on others—especially their local community" (2000, 61). Such activities invite students to learn and then *do* something meaningful with their new knowledge, something research shows is a strong motivator for adolescent boys (Smith and Wilhelm 2002). Following are suggestions for helping students find topics that will catapult them into social action within their school, community, or society at large.

Interview Projects

Have students engage in a brainstorming activity first, listing all essential questions that come to mind from the themes that run through Jimmy's stories. Explain that essential questions are those that "get at matters of deep and enduring understanding" (Wiggins and McTighe 1998, 28). These questions generally have no right or wrong answers and cannot be answered with a word or even a sentence. They are multilayered, often complex inquiries that require reflection and deep thought. For example:

- What are the underlying causes of racism?
- To what extent do foster homes or orphanages provide a loving and supportive environment for children in their care?
- How does society address the drug problem? Are the solutions effective?
- Why are domestic violence and/or gang violence so prevalent in our society, and how can teens help reduce it?
- What makes a "good" prison?
- What is the role of education for today's young people?
- What does it mean to be literate?
- What is the definition of success?

Then, with a partner or in small groups, students choose one question that they would like to investigate. After talking together about the underlying issue framed by the essential question, other questions soon begin to emerge. Students are then ready to discuss who might be able to continue the dialogue with them and help them explore answers, and the interview project is on its way. (See Figure 6–2 for guidelines for interviewing.)

Sometimes, simply having students report their findings to the class will sow the seeds of involvement. When I was in the classroom, I had students complete a "reading/writing/sharing" project each term where students had to create an in-depth literacy project (Lent 2006). One of my students had been reading everything she could find about AIDS because one of her family members had tragically contracted HIV. She found through local community services a young mother who had the disease, interviewed her, and then reported her findings to several classes. No one who heard that presentation will ever think about AIDS again without remembering this student's poignant story.

Community Service Projects

As noted in Chapter 1, community service-learning is cited as a factor that supports whole-school improvement. In fact, research affirms that service-

FIGURE 6–2

Guidelines for Interviewing

1. Students come up with names of people who are knowledgeable about the topic and who might be willing to talk with them. Encourage students to branch out and not always seek "experts." For example, with the very broad question that is posed in the lesson for "The Warden"—"What makes a good prison?"—their list of possible interviewees may include those who served years in large prisons and those who spent one night in the local jail, wardens, parents of people who have served time in jail, young people who have had a parent incarcerated, juvenile detention teachers, students, judges, and those who advocate for prison reform.

2. Students will contact the person or people they wish to interview, telling them the purpose of the interview, what questions they might expect, and asking them how much time they can devote to the interview. Additionally, students should ask interviewees how they want the session conducted: through email, over the phone, in person, or by teleconferencing.

3. Once students know who they are interviewing, they begin the process of generating questions. Have them brainstorm all possible questions related to the topic and then narrow down the list to those that are most applicable. Encourage students to jot down follow-up questions as well and to be flexible enough to change questions if the interview begins going in a new, interesting direction.

4. Allow students to practice interviewing before the actual event by bringing someone into the class, perhaps another teacher, and having students ask questions, jot down answers, and practice the art of follow-up.

5. After students conduct the interview, they will synthesize their information into a publishable format: a column for the local newspaper or school paper, a class booklet on various topics (along with photographs of the interviewees), or a website or wiki on the topic.

6. Have students write thank-you notes to their subjects and make sure they get a copy of the final report to their subjects.

learning has benefits that include improving academic learning and enhancing cultural and racial understanding. And, what's more, student texts produced in community-based writing courses "tend to be more complex and carefully edited than those generated in traditional classrooms" (Newkirk and Kent 2007, 192).

Dawn Stracener cochairs a program at South Valley Academy in Albuquerque, New Mexico, where all students, grades 7–12, go to community placements once a week for three hours. By the time they are seniors, they work individually to analyze community assets and challenges based on a topic they have chosen. They then plan and implement their community service project and present their exhibitions in the spring.

Dawn said that one of the best projects she has seen was on teen dating violence. Alma Flores, a senior in her program, worked with a major community partner to bring awareness to legislators concerning this issue. This student also did a TV show called "Stop the Violence" and educated more than four hundred teens and adults about teen dating violence. During her presentation, Alma said, "Teens are willing to make a difference and I have the potential to achieve what I want" (Stracener 2009).

Other research confirms this story. Sixth graders in an inner-city school were asked to describe what made them feel proud, successful, or creative. They mentioned projects that had "strong social consequences, such as tutoring younger children, learning to make presentations to outside audiences, designing blueprints for playhouses that were to be built by professionals and then donated to preschool programs, and learning to work effectively in groups" (National Research Council 2000, 61). The stories in this text and those in the student book, *Stories from the Edge*, are grounded in themes that could be springboards for community service projects, from penal reform to racial justice to environmental awareness. Have students read the stories with a purpose: How can the ideas and events embedded in the text spur you to action in your community?

Examples of service-learning may include the following.

- Helping a local organization such as a homeless shelter by adopting a family or offering a literacy tutoring service.

- Creating brochures to pass out at grocery stores encouraging the public to donate to the community food bank.

- Constructing informational websites or wikis about issues such as immigration, emotional abuse, or sexually transmitted diseases.

- Writing poetry or short stories about social issues, perhaps modeling pieces after Jimmy's stories and poems. Students could publish a literary magazine containing fiction, poetry, and art that addresses issues often marginalized in schools, and place the magazines in doctor's offices, government buildings, and libraries.

- Speaking or writing to local/state officials or others who may be in a position to foster change. They may also contribute to blogs or join listservs to communicate with others who care about the same issues.

- Creating videos to educate others about issues of importance to teens.

Panel Discussions and Forums

Jimmy's stories are rich with paradoxes culled from a life that few of us could even imagine. Perhaps that is why he often offers splashes of insight that disrupt our complacency. Panel discussions are wonderful ways for students to engage in projects that explore their thinking in front of an audience, an activity that requires listening, communicating, and thinking. It is, after all, the format that made Oprah famous—and every student understands just how it works.

Panel Discussion

To generate a panel discussion based on the stories in this book, have four to six students read the same story and, literature circle style, discuss one or two events, ideas, or themes within the story that elicit thought-provoking dialogue, disparate views, or connections to their world. The students are the "panel" and the rest of the class listens to their discussion. If time allows, class members may ask questions once the panel finishes. In the beginning, the teacher may need to provide a few prompts to get students talking, but often a passage from a story or a few lines from a poem are enough to get the ball rolling.

For example in the short story "The Swing Test That Made Us Men" (page 85) Jimmy writes,

> But here was the most important part of this boyhood ceremony that gave ritual to our coming-of-age in the world—you had to break a bone. Breaking a bone was a symbol of manhood, a badge of honor; it meant you had walked through the fire to prove you were not afraid of pain. And the worse the break, the greater the courage you displayed before the hungry hordes of kids starving for a shot at the swing to prove themselves, too.

The panel discussion that could evolve from this passage might include talking about coming-of-age rituals for today's youth, why pain is so often associated with honor, or the meaning of courage.

The purpose of a panel discussion is not to come to consensus, but to discover new understandings through dialogue. Because the exchange takes place in front of the class, the audience learns to listen attentively, wait to be recognized by the panel discussion leader when and if the time is right, and leave the experience with new insights.

Forums

Forums are often a more public project than panel discussions, but they contain the same elements: analysis of ideas generally derived from text, and thoughtful consideration of others' views. National Issues Forums (NIF) offers resources for educators who want to help their students learn the art of deliberation, where all views are considered, as opposed to debate, where only one side wins. This organization addresses deliberative learning as an approach that emphasizes dialogue, inquiry, and choice making. "Deliberative learners explore complex topics in-depth, consider diverse perspectives on these topics, identify and work through tensions inherent to those views, and attempt to arrive at reasoned judgment" (www.nifi.org). Forums can lead to increased understanding on any topic but, more importantly, they show students how to become responsible participants in civil discourse.

NIF has produced comprehensive booklets of research on many topics of societal concern, such as children and family, education, or civil rights. They will also provide information on how to conduct a forum. Many of the topics listed on page 70 could also be used as forum topics. Racism, for example, could be the topic for a forum that might involve not only students in a school, but also members from the community. (See Figure 6–3 for guidelines for creating a forum on racism.)

Conclusion: Joyful Learning

As teachers, we think about the role of education and the many opportunities it provides but we also must admit that business as usual is simply not working. Too many students are engaging in superficial learning for the sole purpose of passing tests—or, worse, becoming so discouraged and disinterested that they find dropping out a less painful option. We hear in students'

FIGURE 6–3

Guidelines for Creating a Forum on Racism

1. Students will read a variety of texts that address racism, beginning with the stories in this book, with an essential question in mind: What are the underlying causes of racism? Other texts may include biographies, news articles, poetry, or fiction.

2. The class, through small-group discussion, decides on three (or more) broad statements that they feel best answers the question. Options might include the following.

   - Racism is caused by misunderstanding.
   - Racism is caused by stereotyping.
   - Racism is caused by hatred.

3. Students then divide into one of the three groups based upon their beliefs and further analyze the statement—finding examples, making connections to their own experiences, and looking at any available research.

4. Each group will provide at least two moderators who will lead the class through a discussion of their statement. These students will be taught moderating skills during a special session with the teacher.

5. Ground rules are set in place before any dialogue begins, such as

   - Audience members speak only when recognized by a moderator, one at a time.
   - Audience members seek to understand each other and find common ground.
   - Each speaker is allotted no more than three minutes to speak at any one time.
   - Disrespectful behavior will not be permitted.

voices a sense of betrayal when they realize their future often depends on mandates imposed from someone, somewhere, who will never know their individual talents.

Our hearts break when we meet teenagers who tell us they have never once found the exquisite joy in reading or discovered how to shape, as Jimmy says, "another self in the text that is forming" when they write. If even one student walks out of the schoolhouse doors for the last time and has not experienced what it means to care for and connect with peers in a community or become involved in meaningful, challenging learning, that's one too many.

Jimmy and I hope that the stories and lessons that follow will change forever any notion that education is a "boring" necessity kids must endure to have a productive life. We fervently believe that learning is a gift that nurtures and sustains, one that students will receive with gratitude as they come to experience its transformative power.

Further Reading

Drama for Learning: Dorothy Heathcote's Mantle of the Expert Approach to Education (Heathcote 1995)

"Reading Don't Fix No Chevys": Literacy in the Lives of Young Men (Smith and Wilhelm 2002)

Speaking Volumes: How to Get Students Discussing Books—and Much More (Gilmore 2006)

"You Gotta BE the Book" (Wilhelm 2008)

Stories by Jimmy Santiago Baca and Suggestions for Teaching

Jimmy's Introduction

The Journey to Be Loved

I've written more extensively about this in my memoir *A Place to Stand*, but I'd like to give you a snapshot of how it all started—that is, how I learned to read and write when I was in my twenties, and what the journey was like.

The first five years of my life were enveloped in a sweet silence of the prairie and so abundant was silence that I could lose myself for hours playing with pieces of wood, stones, and flowers. The wind whispered to me, shadows urged me to follow them into darker spaces in abandoned barns and shacks. I hurled headlong into the depth of light that shone with a dull density in the grasshopper's wings, and it seemed a solitary angel's voice sang all my wounds open and squeezed from them the infection and healed my pain by morning's end.

With my imagination so intact and volatile, casting on inanimate things a vigorous life of their own, I was anything but lonely. All things reflected their dreams to me, and induced in me a hypnotic enchantment where I re-created and shaped my perspective on life.

If I saw an old man pushing a cart of pots and pans he had repaired and was trying to sell, he became a prince giving away secret maps to the fabled fairy-tale lands. A grasshopper became God in green wings and large eyes and antennae. A horny toad, a warrior armored for battle. Ants were my serfs and I whirled in the dust and cacti crawling in the dirt trying to scare a quail. I became Pavarotti, singing in my own romantic opera on a stage inhabited by cedar and juniper trees that sat spellbound listening to my tragic and ecstatic tale.

I compressed all life into a common pebble that I tossed in the air and pocketed because I liked its colors or markings.

It was all pretending because pretending was a way to deny seeing my dad and mom fight last night. My own make-believe world blocked out the other world of drunk uncles and money-hungry cousins and fights about poverty.

It was when I was five years old, after my parents had left us with grandma, that grandma said she could not take care of my sister, brother, and me and she informed us that authorities would arrive within days to take my brother and me to an orphanage.

With that information my pretend world shattered.

But it wasn't as bad as I expected.

I learned to understand a new reality through the eyes of movie characters like Pinocchio, Bambi, and Ben-Hur, and in the classroom at the orphanage, I would sit by the window and doodle in the margins of my Dick and Jane book. I never learned to read very well and my ability to express myself was negligible at best. Books had very little to do with my life for the first eighteen years.

I was an impulsive, idealistic follower. I thought everyone had the answer to how the world really worked except me. I was wrong but I didn't know it because everyone seemed opinionated and boasted about their wisdom. I'd go with anyone to do almost anything they asked; as long as they led, I was their guy, there to give support and show my loyalty.

The orphanage was run by Franciscan nuns and they didn't put much importance on education, at least not as much as converting our souls and making sure we grew into pious Christians.

I enjoyed enormously singing in the choir, and I belted out Latin lyrics to hymns as if the good Lord sat a foot away from me midair listening to my beautiful homage. I loved working the barn animals, milking the cows, feeding the pigs, riding the back of trucks, and going around town picking up donated shoes and day-old donuts and bread; wrecking havoc on the playground with our incredibly dangerous games.

But I had problems with saints. Kneeling in the pews every morning and praying to them? Ugh. Especially knowing that Father Gallagher was molesting certain kids, and some of the younger nuns were carrying on sexual liaisons with other kids. And then there were the gruesome Stations of the Cross that flanked the pews and hung on the walls surrounding us.

All this made me wonder about the world and confused me even more. Still, I endured the discrepancies and lounged in my happiness like an old dog before a fireplace in winter. That is, until Sister Pauline, the Superior, informed me she was sending me to Boys Town.

I ran away that same evening. I begged my older brother to come with me but he was scared, so I hugged him, and he stood there looking after me as I disappeared into the night. Had I known at the time I would not see my brother for a year after that night, I probably wouldn't have left him.

Not knowing a person in the world beyond the fence boundary of the orphanage, nor anything about the world beyond, I clambered over the fence, and crawled on hands and knees until I was far enough away to stand and run along the ditch. I headed in the direction where I thought my maternal grandma lived.

I found her place but she had been moved and I was homeless. I became a street kid for the next seven years, joined a group of other homeless kids, going in and out of the Boys Detention Home, doing time at Montessa Park—a gladiator school that prepared teenagers for prison—and months at different intervals in the county jail for fighting, burglary, and possession of drugs.

It was a small leap to prison. On the cusp of turning nineteen, I was convicted of possession of heroin with the intent to sell and sentenced to five to ten years in a maximum-security prison without chance of parole, to do day for day with no good time allowed.

I was physically stopped and I needed to be; if I hadn't been, I am absolutely certain I'd be dead. I was on a death mission for years, partying, getting drunk, doing drugs, hanging out with the wrong guys—in every respect, when I look back on those days, I see a kid, yes—innocent and beautiful and lost and uneducated and with no family or real friends, and because of that, with a hidden suicide wish.

In prison, however, I wanted to change that and get an education and see if I could improve my life, even from behind bars and walls. But the prison administration refused to let me attend school to get my GED and I retaliated by refusing to work or go along with the prison rules. This branded me as a troublemaker. I was given indefinite disciplinary punishment and locked down in administrative segregation, in a dungeon with the most brutal and cruelest gangbangers, where for the next three years I taught myself to read and write.

I wanted to learn to read and write because it was a tool that would help me understand people and systems—why people do what they do.

Why was it that my family was so poor and dysfunctional? What mechanism was in the system that a judge wouldn't even consider giving me a chance to help myself? Why, when looking through the bars of my prison cell, was it that all those people were free and I was not? Books had the answers, and I was going to find them. I was determined to solve my dilemma myself. I had depended on what people said and suggested for far too long. Now, my life and my role in the world would be shaped and molded by my own ideas and feelings.

The driving force to educate myself never slowed or relented. I devoured books. I wrote my first letters to people, I kept a journal, wrote poems, and miraculously the power of literacy took hold and dug in and embedded itself in my heart. I became known to myself and loved who I started to know in me. Through the mist and darkness, through the tears and misguided intentions, through the anger and despair that entangled me for so many years, Jimmy was emerging—a strong, beautiful Jimmy, with the growing capacity to think and analyze the world beyond, and to make courageous choices interacting in that world.

It was extraordinary to have this power to name things, to study my past and understand why I did what I did. The destructive forces at play in my life stopped and positive and creative forces poured in, transforming me into a formidable human being capable of healing old wounds and forgiving enemies. Every morning on awaking, I eagerly moved forward into a new landscape where a future awaited me.

I was not going to be exiled like a leper or driven from society like a low-life criminal. I was not a criminal, I was a human being trying to understand the world, and I learned I could not do it without educating myself. As a human being, I suffered through horrible times where I almost gave up. I couldn't go anymore—I wanted to pick up old habits and resume my violent response to the world. Someone disrespected me, stole something of mine, said something bad to me and I found myself wanting to throw the books away and deal with the punk on the yard and show him you don't earn a reputation with me so other convicts will look up to you—no, you get a beat-down.

But I realized this was the coward's way, and this way never worked for me. Now, I realized, I had an opportunity to give myself a fighting chance to make my dreams come true and I went for it, with as much gusto and fearlessness as I ever had going for anything I'd wanted in my past life.

It was all going to be different now and I was going to make it happen myself. If I had to pace my cell for twenty years to learn how to read, I would do it. Thank God it didn't take that long. Restlessly, when I started I paced for hours in my cell reading aloud, writing on a tablet for hours, reading all through the night, month after month, until finally, I could compose my first letter.

Not only did I go through enormous changes, but suddenly the hard-core fighters and warriors around me started looking at me and treating me with renewed respect. They wanted me to speak for them, to answer their questions, and help them solve their problems by helping them understand their own feelings.

I remember with joy what an incredible power it was to be able to express myself, not just read and write, but convey my ideas to another convict, to have their respect because I was smart, to have them depend on me to write their letters home, to have them look up to me because I had done it, improved myself, done something they wanted to do but felt they couldn't do.

I never suspected in my craziest reveries that I would eventually become a poet. Nor could I allow myself to imagine that the poems I was writing down in the dungeon would be published one day.

I had my first book of poems published by Louisiana State University and shortly after that one, ten more books followed. I wrote and executive-produced *Blood In/Blood Out*, the feature movie produced by Hollywood Pictures. I went on to write novels, short story collections, more poetry, essays, more movies. But as important as all of this is, including my thirty-two awards, rising above all these achievements, is that I am now educated. I went to school, got my BA and master's, and was honored with a PhD.

And greater than even that, I have a lovely family, and my five children are very proud of and love their father. That was all I ever wanted, to be respected and loved.

The Swing Test That Made Us Men

It was a test alright and it cut the boys from the men. At the orphanage, there were only two swings for twelve hundred kids and every kid on the playground yearned for the opportunity to ride the swing because it symbolized much more than just a swing.

First of all, you had to earn your turn. When a kid was carted off or simply tired of swinging, everyone raced to get it. Lee Walker was the fastest kid in the orphanage so he had no trouble getting to it first.

The only problem was he was running out of bones to break.

Let me explain. Say you got to the swing first. You had to pump your legs and thrust your shoulders forward to get as high as you could. There was absolutely no compromise when it came to height, and once you reached the highest point in your swing, you had to bail out. You bailed out a few times like a jet pilot testing his parachute, and then went for a flip.

Don't kid yourself—every boy on the playground had their antennae tuned to you and they were clocking your every move and appraising the craft and style with which you flipped midair and landed.

But here was the most important part of this boyhood ceremony that gave ritual to our coming-of-age in the world—you had to break a bone. Breaking a bone was a symbol of manhood, a badge of honor; it meant you had walked through the fire to prove you were not afraid of pain. And the worse the break, the greater the courage you displayed before the hungry hordes of kids starving for a shot at the swing to prove themselves, too.

But there was another reason. Breaking a bone was important because only then could you join other warriors in the infirmary and get a hug from Sister Theobaldus. She was this huge three hundred and fifty–pound German nun and nestling your head between her enormous breasts was the closest thing to mothering most of us kids would ever know. In short, her breasts were Heaven on Earth and kids were willing to risk life and limb for a moment between God's gift to homeless kids.

Once we made it to the infirmary and indulged in the luxurious dream-bosom, we were in store for another treat—the lemon drop candies. Sister Theobaldus reached her massive paw into her apron pocket and pulled out a gob of lemon drops, which we all believed hastened our healing.

And while we sucked on lemon drops and grazed against the white nurse's uniform containing the eighth wonder of the world, Sister Theobaldus helped us into our pajamas and settled us into one of the beds.

There, we could relax in newfound glory among those in the other beds, feeling for a few days like one of the luckiest kids in the world.

Suggestions for Teaching

Jimmy describes a swing test where broken bones symbolize manhood, with the accompanying reward of feeling loved and special, if only for a few days. Help students write about their own "swing test," a time in life when they felt they had to prove to others who they were—or who they wanted to be. This activity may be one that students do not want to share, as the incident they describe may be personal or even embarrassing. The purpose of this writing is not necessarily to produce a finished piece but, rather, to help students analyze past experiences with a writer's eye.

Sample Lesson

1. Have students think about a time they were scared to do something but did it anyway to prove themselves to someone else—maybe a rite of passage or a coming-of-age moment in their own lives. Explain

that they may even have felt what they were doing was not right, but the rewards of others' admiration or acceptance were too great to overcome. Students may brainstorm with a partner or in a small group to target a memory they want to write about.

2. Help students get started by having them freewrite about the events of a specific memory. Once they have the events in place, ask them to explore *why* they took the action they are describing as well as the tension between rewards and risks.

3. Jimmy concludes his story by saying the boys felt like the luckiest kids in the world for a few days. Encourage students to pay attention to the way they end their piece. Are they able to conclude as definitively as Jimmy did or were the feelings about themselves more complicated? They may want to reflect about how their perspective has changed over time.

Beyond the Classroom

Suggest that students take their writer's notebooks and visit a playground after school. They should sit quietly and observe small children as they swing. Do they jump from the swings? Are other kids waiting in line to swing? What do they call out to their friends? Do any of them seem to want to impress others? How might Jimmy compare the scene the students observe to his own childhood memory of the "The Swing Test"?

The Magic Marble

When it was announced that a marble tournament was to be held and that the champion would go on to the regional competition, and if he advanced, then on to the state finals, my friends and I sat in the ditch away from the others and dreamed ourselves the marble champs.

We crushed dry leaves and rolled them in comic book paper into cigarettes and smoked them. We were big guys even at seven, a month or so from being adults. It was either Peanut Head or Big Noodle who came up with a plan on how to achieve our dream.

In short, we figured Cavalo's glass eye would do it for us; that is, we simply had to direct it into the ring and it would knock the marbles out of the circle. We thought the glass eye could see the marbles and so would never miss. We would not only win, we would make history and the Guinness Book of World Records for the most marbles ever hit without a miss.

But how to get the eye from Cavalo?

Cavalo was a medieval dragon of a man. There were four brand-new dorms recently built, 100s for the toddlers and infants; 200s for the slightly older, 300 and 400s for older boys. My friends and I were in the 300s, and Cavalo also slept in this dorm.

He got up earlier than us kids, trudged like one of Solzhenitsyn's Russian peasant prisoners in the semidark to the subterranean boiler room and stoked the fires to get the radiators knocking to warm the classrooms before school. Sometimes I would pass the boiler room and catch a glimpse of him below—a grizzly ogre, with Popeye forearms, hair stiff and bristly as barbwire, a permanent scowl on his face, and a perennial stream of yellowish mucus dripping from the glass eye socket.

Last time he glowered when he glanced up at me, and it scared me enough that I made it a point to avoid passing the boiler room for months.

Every night, Cavalo took his glass eye out and placed it in a glass of water on his bed stand next to his cot. With his eye out, he looked fierce, the eyelids of his socket shrunken back into tight whorls of flesh seamed with mucus.

But we did have to get that eye and the marble tournament was drawing near.

We decided that we would wait until he went to sleep and crawl over to his bed and pluck the glass eye from the water. He could always get another glass eye and we would win the tournament and, as they say, all's well that ends well.

The kids in the dorms finally went to bed and the nun who had her own enclosed room in a corner of the dorm said good night and turned off the lights. We waited a good hour until we could hear kids snoring, farting, and moaning.

Big Noodle and Coo-Coo Clock crept over to my bunk. Soon Peanut Head arrived and they all took their stations as planned. Coo-Coo Clock was posted at Sister Juanita's room and ready to alert us if he heard her moving about. Big Noodle and Peanut Head stationed themselves at the head of the bunk rows as lookouts.

I crawled over to Cavalo's cot, dipped my fingers into the glass, and scooped out the magic glass eye. I turned and saw a blurred object sailing past me and attributed the blue, dark object to my own imagination. As everyone knows, your sight plays tricks on you in the dark.

Anyway, it wasn't my imagination, it was a boot that someone had hurled through the air and it hit Cavalo in the head. He roused from his sleep and rose out of bed in a mean roar, growling for his eye. Sister Juanita awoke and came out and turned on the dorm light, and I froze as Cavalo loomed over me like a mythic one-eyed giant.

He bent down and his face came within inches of mine. "WHERE'S MY EYE?!" he bellowed.

Just before the lights had gone on I had managed, as much as I was repulsed by it, to put the eye in my mouth. I had no choice. I intended to spit it out later but it didn't work out that way.

Cavalo scared me so much, I swallowed it.

Sister Juanita pulled me by the ear into the bathroom where for the next hour she made me swallow saltwater and puke, puke at least a hundred times, until the marble came rolling out onto the floor.

So much for the marble tournament. As punishment we had to wash all five hundred windows in the buildings, and we missed the tournament. I still wonder from time to time who threw that boot.

Suggestions for Teaching

Students will enjoy reading this lively story and discussing how Jimmy has used a bit of gallows humor to make Cavalo come to life. Help them explore literary elements such as characterization and figurative language as they create their own Cavalo through the following activity.

Sample Lesson

1. Read "The Magic Marble" aloud to students, using your voice to full effect as students enjoy the tale.

2. Give each student a copy of the piece and have them underline any words or phrases that describe the character Cavalo. (If they have the student book, *Stories from the Edge*, and you don't want them to mark it up, they can use sticky notes to jot down the words or phrases and tab the pages.) Allow them to share with a partner.

3. Lead a discussion, asking students why they thought Jimmy chose particular words or metaphors to describe Cavalo, such as "Popeye." Ask them how changing only a few words would alter the image Baca created in their minds. For example, in the phrase "with Popeye fore-arms, hair stiff and bristly as barbwire" how would their mental picture of Cavalo have been different if Jimmy had written "hair stiff as *steel wool*" or "hair stiff as *porcupine quills*"?

4. Have each student write her own description of Cavalo. Provide the following sentence to get them started: "Sometimes I would pass the boiler room and catch a glimpse of him below." Encourage them to be creative, perhaps creating a completely different type of person. Allow students to share their creations first with a partner and then with the rest of the class. As they read, write words or phrases from their descriptions on the board that are especially good.

Beyond the Classroom

Ask students to find a character online or in a movie/TV show—or think about someone from their own lives—and describe the character. They may create a jot list of physical characteristics and then "show" the character by noting examples of how the person speaks or behaves. The next day in class, have students work with a partner, paying attention to specific words or metaphors as they revise their piece to create an image of the character that is compelling.

Wells Market

There wasn't a day that passed that I didn't yearn for a visit from my mother or grandmother. During ordinary days, it was bad enough that they had never visited me, but when holidays rolled around, my longing intensified because it was a time when many families came to visit other kids in the orphanage.

At Christmastime there was so much festive excitement in the air that I couldn't sleep. I woke at 5:00 AM to attend mass after a fitful night of tossing and turning, and my first thought as my eyes lifted to greet the daylight was, *Is today the day my mother or grandmother are coming to see me?*

Still, with hope nestled in my heart on the verge of bursting forth from its star shell, I lunged into the pre-Christmas craziness at St. Anthony's orphanage.

It was the coolest holiday of all, not only because the nuns decked out the chapel with a thousand mythic candles and wreaths and freshly cut flowers, but also because mass services were rendered in Latin and I got to sing in the choir and blast out Gregorian chants, which I absolutely loved. I knew if I sang loud enough, God would hear me and grant my wish for a visit.

In the classroom, I drew and cut out snowflakes, snowmen, and Santas and taped them to the windows, spraying white snow hills for sleighs to ride over, stringing up lightbulbs, and running glittering blue and red bunting around the window frames.

We'd make and sell hundreds of *farolitos*, paper lunch sacks we'd fill with two scoops of sand and a small candle placed on top. People lined them on fence tops, rooftops, and walkways and on Christmas Eve they lit the candles. It transformed the night into a biblical fairy tale.

The chilly days smacked with excitement, games, and the flavor of special holiday foods. I had a cardboard flap I'd torn off a box and each afternoon I lined up with other kids to slide on the ice that covered the courtyard cobblestone.

In the auditorium we played the game Murder in the Dark. In this game, a ball made of old socks is set on the floor between the two teams. The object is to grab the sock ball and carry it over the opponent's line, called the end zone. This would be easy in itself, but you have to do it as someone flicks the lights on and off. If you're caught moving when the lights are on, you're out. The excitement of the game came when the lights were off. You could punch and slug and push some kid you didn't like but when the lights went on many of us were busted in the act of hitting or being hit.

When not playing Murder in the Dark, we got to watch movies like *Ben-Hur*, *Big Valley*, *Miracle on 57th Street*, and *The Christmas Story*, with Charlton Heston parting the Red Sea, and the three kings following a star to find baby Jesus asleep in the manger. And when the auditorium wasn't being used to watch movies, the nuns provided entertainment for us by inviting special guests.

A sorority from the University of New Mexico visited once. Instead of luxuriating in the attention and playing dumb games, I wanted more exciting distractions, so me and a few other pirates headed up to the condemned third floor of the main building, where the girls had stashed their coats and purses.

We felt we had beached on an island of lost treasures as we scavenged through their purses, dumping out the contents and pocketing lipsticks, panties, photos, nylons, money, and other precious valuables that could be used for barter with other kids and the nuns.

There were some nuns who would kiss us for candy, others who would dance with us for a mascara case; still others, if we brought them a new pair of nylons, invited us to their rooms at night. No matter what form it materialized in, we were starved for female affection and we found it in the young nuns who were also famished for intimacy, even if they had to compromise and engage with a boy younger than they might have wished for.

After we had pillaged the coat and purse room, taken the loot to the barn and hidden it under the haystack, we returned to the auditorium. I should have listened to my friends' warning not to bring anything inside but I couldn't help it—I was a show-off.

I brought back a purse to show the other kids how special I was, how brave and bad I was. After showing it to a few kids and getting what I wanted—a bunch of blazing *oooh*s and *wow*s, their eyes wide with admiration conferring heroic status on me—I stuffed the evidence behind a radiator and, intent on getting it later, forgot about it.

The stench of melting plastic filled the auditorium and soon smoke rose from behind the radiator. One of the nuns plucked out a half-melted purse and demanded to know who the guilty one was. Meanwhile, the sorority girls had rushed out of the auditorium to check on their belongings and returned aghast over the burglary.

The nuns lined us up and sternly paced back and forth with arms crossed behind their backs. They wanted an admission of guilt, and ordered the immediate return of the purses and contents, threatening to punish everyone if the guilty party didn't step forward.

I confessed, but I didn't tell them that I had saved a bunch of lipsticks and mascara cases for my mother in case she came during Christmas to see me. I put them in a special hiding place. And when they sent the older boys to retrieve our stash, I was pleased that I had something left to redeem a bit of the pain from the beating that was coming.

Room Number 5 was the hated and feared room where kids were sent to get a spanking. I had visited there many times. I had been there for raiding the kitchen cart when it came rumbling down the long hallway toward the dining room, and my friends and I would leap down from the staircase and load up on the hotdogs and cake and butter. Other times I was caught stuffing myself with cherry-filled chocolates, extorted from nuns carrying on secret affairs with kids. But mostly I was punished for the many times I had run away to see my grandma.

I ran to my grandma because I knew where she was, whereas my mother's life was a mystery. My mother had vanished into thin air and I was never told where she lived or what she was doing. But I was certain she would come for me; I figured she was planning our reunion just as I was.

After the stinging from the spanking numbed and I could toddle again, I walked into the chapel at five o'clock as we did every morning. Besides the lipsticks and mascara I had saved for my mother, the chapel with its wreaths, candles, serene nativity scene, and the singing of Christmas hymns in the choir loft seemed to alleviate my soreness.

I couldn't wait to be outside again, on my knees in the sand pile bagging *farolitos*, snapping out a paper sack and pouring in two scoops of sand and a candle, loading up the civilian trunks of endless cars waiting to purchase enough sacks to decorate their houses. Then, we would ride all over the city in the back of the truck, emptying the endless parking-lot containers of donations to the orphanage, and ride back on a mountain of shoes or clothes piled in the back of the truck. Some days we'd hit bakeries and grocery stores and load the truck with pastries and bread; other days we'd hit farmer's markets and load the truck with blemished fruits.

But no matter the excursions and adventure, to alleviate my worrisome yearning for my mother, I snuck into Father Gallagher's rectory and drank wine, and when I got drunk enough, I stole a few holy wafers from the chalice in his rectory and ate them as I promised eternal devotion to God if he only brought my mom to visit me.

But my mother never came.

Perhaps it was jumping into the arctic swimming pool in the morning during winter that made my immune system so resilient, or playing with Lincoln Logs in the playroom and napping on the floor with a cold draft coming under the doors, or playing on the teeter–totter while it was snowing, or baseball during windy days, or any number of other things I did. But as immune as I was, my heart still felt the touch of sorrow and folded in on itself like a butterfly's time to die in winter, curled up to endure its own solitude during such a communally happy time.

Months earlier, I had run away from the orphanage to plunder gifts that I intended to give to my grandma. To break into a secondhand store with nice hats, I had climbed up to the roof using the fire escape stairwell, kicked out the air-conditioning ductwork, and slid into the store. Once in, I loaded up on dresses, shoes, hats, and panties for my grandma, then threw the bag holding everything up through the hole I'd made in the ceiling and leaped after it. Grabbing the sides of the ceiling, I kicked my legs up and hooked my feet over the edge.

Just as I was ready to pull myself up, a police cruiser pulled up and two officers entered. They swept the place with their flashlights and, satisfied everything was okay, prepared to leave when the pennies I had stuffed in my pocket from the cash register began raining down on the floor. Their strobe lights swept the dark again until they found the waterfall of pennies and trailed it up to me, hanging upside down like a monkey, my eyes staring down at them.

They had arrested me before for running away and that night they were the ones who told me that my grandmother had been taken to a place for old people, where she would be tended to because she was too old and couldn't take care of herself. They said she had a disease called Alzheimer's, but it wasn't hurting her. They took me to see where she was living, but we only passed by the place. I wasn't allowed inside.

When the other kids' grandmothers came to visit them, I waited day after day at the outside gate by the Virgin Mary Grotto hoping my grandma might drive up with a bag of holiday goodies too, but that never happened.

Once, I went with my friend Coo-Coo Clock to the Blue Room, the room for visits, and I saw him and his grandmother and others in their chairs. The kids were unwrapping new head scarves, slipping on new gloves and coats, and piled on their laps were bags filled with toys and candies. My friends shared their candies with me, but it wasn't the same as having a family member visit.

It was maybe a week from Christmas, when the nuns got us all together and bused us to the zoo park to play.

When the teams were chosen for a football game, I was selected by one of the most popular kids in the orphanage—Johnny La'O. He was the biggest and strongest and everybody feared him, even though he was nice and seldom threw his weight around. He was not a bully; he was as compassionate and heroic as Ben-Hur was in the black-and-white movies we watched on Friday nights in the auditorium.

Anyway, he chose me, and I guess knowing that I didn't have anyone visit me for Christmas, he looked directly at me in the huddle and said he was going to throw the bomb to me. That meant a long Hail Mary pass.

And I was going to catch it and run for a touchdown. At least that was what I had imagined would happen.

When the football was hiked I dashed as fast as I could, as far as my little legs would carry me and I turned and saw the football sailing my way. My entire focus was on it. Catching it was the only thing that mattered in the whole world. I reached out and I had it. Within seconds, I imagined myself galloping for a touchdown, then lofted on my teammates' shoulders as they carried me victoriously to our team bench.

Instead, everything went black.

In a tiny, white room, my spirit hovered over an operating room lamp, observing doctors below. There they stood, working on my physical body, which was reclined on an operating gurney while the doctors wrapped my head in gauze and the nuns surrounding me clasped hands, clutching rosaries as they prayed.

Disembodied, I was floating in a space with no time or place. I had just been operated on. And I heard words like *coma* and *chin* and *tree* and phrases about God saving me. Looking down at myself, I wondered how I got on the gurney and into the hospital. I wasn't worried, I was curious.

That out-of-body experience was only temporary, perhaps because I was so heavily medicated. I'm still puzzled by how I ended up back at the orphanage. But there I was, hours or days later—I can't remember—standing in line with the other kids with a huge gauze bandage circling my head. The gauze was wrapped under my chin too, and I looked like a huge, walking marshmallow.

I don't remember much about that time, except it was close to Christmas and I wanted to see my grandma, the only person in the world besides my mother who made living a magical experience, and who could redeem the perpetual, throbbing misery I was in. I would willingly, even gratefully, accept the sorrow of life if I'd just be allowed to see my grandma once a year during Christmas.

A week later I was in line in the auditorium when Santa came and gave out red stockings stuffed with fruits and nuts and a few *ho-ho-ho*s. I could tell he was a fake Santa because I could see the beard bands and the discolored hair under his hat. He had yellow teeth, red-veined eyes from drinking too much the night before, and lint caught in the hair tufts around his ears.

After Santa left we all lined up again to meet three huge black men, ushered in by the nuns with pontifical decorum. Each kid shook the hand of the one giant flanked by two smaller ones and moved on until my turn came and the black giant leaned down and bellowed in a baritone voice, "What happened little buddy? Somebody hit you?"

I shook my head no and wanted to say I ran into a tree but I couldn't move my mouth or jaw that well. His interest pleased me. He gently caressed my chin with a big, black, thick finger, then turned to one of his two assistants beside him and said, "Joe, go to the car and bring the gloves."

His errand man came right back and gave these two big red boxing gloves to him.

In a voice low as a paddle in water, he leaned down and said, "My name is Sonny Liston. I am the heavyweight champion of the world. I won the title fight with these gloves. They have magic; they can help you win fights, make you a winner, a champion. Here."

He held the gloves out to me.

They were as big as my torso, shoulders, and arms, and I hugged them to me like they were real teddy bears. I took a chair in the auditorium with the other kids, and sensed these gloves were big business; they meant something big.

Johnny La'O came up behind me and whispered, "I'll give you whatever you want for those, Jimmy, anything," he said. Then added, with passion, "Please . . . *please.*"

I thought for a second and then I uttered with great difficulty, "I-want-to-see-my-grandma . . . and-you-can-have-the-gloves."

That night, when everyone was asleep in the dorm, as arranged between Johnny La'O and me and following his instructions, I snuck out and ran to the fields by the public road. There, I waited in the alfalfa until I heard a motorcycle drive up and idle by the road shoulder and field.

I dashed to the motorcycle and hopped on the back and the driver took off.

"Where to?" he yelled back at me.

I used my hands to motion him directions until we arrived at the old folks' house where my grandma was living. He parked and we went inside.

At first I was kind of disoriented because I had never seen her in this place. The police had driven me by, but I had never been in.

Tonight, I went inside and I saw my grandma in the corner. She was the only white-skinned woman; the rest were old blacks, kind of lounging and ambling aimlessly, standing and lolling, moving slowly to nowhere.

I approached my grandma. "Grandma, Grandma . . ." I called her even though it hurt my head to speak.

She turned and squinted at me. After a moment she blurted out angrily, "Get away! You stole everything, get away! Get out!"

She was referring to her own children, and she called me by the name of one of her older sons. They had stripped her of her land and money and thrown her into this old-age hell-home.

She swung and hit me with her cane. Then swung and hit me again.

I was so hurt that a part of me recoiled in horror and I wanted to end the world. I wanted to rewind my life and before it started, light a match that would burn the world down. This was my pain, but instead of the world burning outside, inside my head my world was a burnt and charcoaled landscape where only night existed and ashes blew continually under the blood red moon called my heart.

My friend tugged at my arm and told me, "Let's go! Let's go! She's going to hit you on the chin and that's going to be bad—she doesn't know who you are Jimmy, she's insane, she's gone crazy."

I followed him out. I felt like throwing up, like I had swallowed poison.

We got on the bike and returned to the orphanage.

The next day, Johnny La'O, knowing what happened, said he had a surprise for me.

I met him on the playground and he led me across the fields, away from the orphanage. I thought we were running away together, that we were going to live with the many girlfriends he had out there on the streets.

But we weren't.

We entered Wells Market, a store as famous in the imagination of children as the North Pole at Christmas. Very rarely did the kids ever make it this far away from the orphanage, and even fewer got to go inside Wells, a storybook store with legendary shelves of candies that blinded one's heart to all else in life.

Only the older kids risked their lives to come to Wells Market, and on their return all we youngsters ringed them as they talked about the aisles brimming with exotic toys and candies.

Now, I saw, and it was true. The store contained all the candies in the world, the shining jewels that sparkled in every kid's dreams.

When I left Wells Market that afternoon, carrying a paper sack filled with fizzies, lollipops, chips, gum, and much more, I was reeling with unspeakable joy. I was numb with ecstasy.

Sure, other kids had parents and homes and grandmas, but now *I* had been to Wells Market. Word got around fast. I was the most famous kid in the world that day. Kids mobbed me as a hero—I had made the perilous journey and returned safe, laden with gold and stories of high adventure, stories that I made up about almost being shot by a rabid farmer protecting his chili garden and how I'd been chased by wild dogs.

That day, like a seasoned politician, I leveraged the candy I handed out. For two scoops, Chief, a big Navajo, let me poke Big Oscar's balls with a stick. Big Oscar was the ribbon-winning state fair champion pig, as big as a truck. Chief typically charged us a dinner dessert to poke Oscar in the balls. This activated Oscar's penis, which slid out from its black pouch of flesh. Little by little the pencil-thin penis appeared and elongated four feet out, a skinny red worm. I also bartered my way onto a go-cart team.

But the best part was being allowed admittance that night to a once-in-a-lifetime viewing of Sister Rita, a kid's girlfriend, in a bathing suit in her room. Sister Rita's room was lit up with candles, and she came out in a bathing suit and turned and smiled. I sat on the couch drooling, stuffing my mouth with candies, until she paused and sat next to me.

Then she held me in her arms like a mother and rocked me.

It was the greatest Christmas ever.

Suggestions for Teaching

In this adventure story, the young Jimmy, much like the legendary Tom Sawyer, goes on escapades that are both heartbreaking and heartwarming.

The truth is transparent throughout the story, however. The lonely boy is sublimating his desire for his mother and grandmother with experiences that bring him momentary relief from his painful longing—to singularly belong to someone. Help students find the underlying themes through the following activity.

Sample Lesson

1. Ask students to reread the story with these questions in mind:
   - What is Jimmy's purpose in writing this story?
   - What is it you think Jimmy wants his readers to understand?

2. Have students read the story silently, noting with highlighters or sticky notes any line or paragraph that students deem important. You might ask them to find only five "important" places to help them focus. Place students in small groups and ask them to share their thoughts.

3. Next, have students write questions about parts of the story they highlighted, either individually or with a partner. Encourage them to write questions that go deeper than low-level comprehension questions, questions that may even be unanswerable. For example, the last line in this story is "It was the happiest Christmas ever" and students may mark this part as important. Questions might include:
   - Why was it the happiest Christmas ever?
   - Was Jimmy happier now than when he was with his family?
   - How could he be happy when he had experienced such trauma while visiting his grandmother?
   - How would Jimmy define happiness at the beginning of the story? At the end?

4. Have students return to their groups. Assign a recorder and a facilitator. Then, ask students to share their questions with the group and discuss how Jimmy might answer the questions.

5. Finally, each group should come up with what they believe is the most important idea Jimmy wanted to communicate to his readers, his purpose for writing the story. The recorder should write this on chart paper or on the board. Compare the responses from different groups as a springboard for deeper discussion.

Beyond the Classroom

Wells Market is the symbolic North Pole, the place where children find delights unimaginable—gifts that multiply into increased status, gifts that can be bartered for privilege, gifts that return time and again in dreams. Have students explore their own Wells Market by writing in their journals about a place that symbolizes all they could ever desire. Some personal writing is best done in private, perhaps at home. Tell students they may do what they wish with this piece—place it in their writing folders, keep it in their own private journals, or share it with someone they trust.

Eleven Cents

Over the years I have met dozens of women who call themselves *curanderas*—spiritual healers—but they all fell short of being truly genuine and authentic. They were usually middle-aged women claiming to be artists but secretly working through their own traumatic experiences, usually caused by a male lover. They were hapless Frida Kahlo look-alikes in long skirts and blouses, professing to be consumed by mystical connections to the spirit world.

Their aura said that their sole purpose in life was to suffer so they might heal others by sacrificing themselves. Only the curanderas were privy to the divine answers they passed on to those who came for counseling. The curandera would answer the questions and the seeker would be given direction and purpose in life.

About a year ago, I picked up two young Chicanos who work in the film industry in Los Angeles from Albuquerque's West Side and we headed down to the university area soundstage to meet a renowned curandera to participate in her blessing circle. I wanted to meet her because I had heard she had powerful prayers and it was a time in my life when I was searching for someone who could help revitalize my depressed spirit. I was intrigued by the stories I'd heard of her and secretly yearned for a genuine healer woman. I needed strong prayers in my life.

On the way there my two Chicano friends were hungry, so we pulled into Wendy's on 4th Street and called out our burger order and idled to the drive-up window.

© 2010 by Jimmy Santiago Baca, from *Adolescents on the Edge* by Jimmy Santiago Baca and ReLeah Cossett Lent. Portsmouth, NH: Heinemann.

A short, dark Mexican repeated our order and I nodded, opening my palm to take the money from my two passengers, then I handed it to the Mexican at the window.

"You're eleven cents short," he said.

The two Chicanos leaned forward to be heard better by the Mexican.

"Come on dude," Val said, "it's only eleven cents, man."

Eddy added, "Let it go. We're one people. We'd do the same for you."

"Give each other breaks, man. Don't hassle us over eleven cents."

But the Mexican was having none of it. "Nobody gave *me* a break when I came here. I went without eating for days. Nobody gave me even a piece of bread."

"Yeah," Val argued, "but that wasn't *us*. This is bull. Eleven cents? You kidding me?"

"No kidding anybody. Pay or you're not getting anything."

Eddy went into a rage, started hollering at him, "You punk! Who do you think you are? You don't even belong here in this country! Go back home, kissing up to the white man."

"You ain't nothing but a sellout, vato," Val yelled.

But he was adamant and refused to hand over the bags of fries, sodas, and burgers.

"Let me out! I'm going to show this dude how we do business here," Val said.

"Why should I give you a break?" the Mexican in the window cried out. "No one, not one person, gave me anything, nothing, when I came here, not a penny—I had to earn everything I got. No one ever gave me a hamburger. No one gave me a hamburger when I came here! No one! I had to pay for everything."

This enraged the two Chicanos even more. Any connection between his suffering and theirs, between what happened to the Mexican when he came to America and how it mattered in this scene with the burgers and eleven cents—they couldn't see it.

I pulled eleven cents out of my pocket and handed it to him and took the bags for Val and Eddy. They grumbled at him, cursed at him, spat with disgust at his revolting subservience to the gringo boss.

I drove across the street and ordered fries, burgers, and soda from McDonald's, and then looped back and came around again to the drive-up window.

"What the hell are you doing?" the Mexican said when he saw us. "Do you have a gun? I'm not afraid of you."

"I don't have a gun. I just came back to say I'm sorry for the way you were treated when you came here. I wish it hadn't been that way. I wish you had been given respect and help. We all deserve that."

I paused and looked in his fearful eyes. "I wanted to give you this burger, fries, and soda, on me, as my way of saying I'm sorry."

Stunned, he stood there blinking and trying to register it mentally, not believing what I was saying for a second, absolutely certain that this was some kind of setup to hurt him.

"What's going on?" he said suspiciously. "You trying to pull something?"

There was no convincing him.

"I'm going to leave this here, and again I'm sorry. Have a good night."

"Whoa, whoa, what are you doing?" Val said. "I'll eat those. Don't give it to that punk."

I turned around and looked at Val.

"He's not a *punk*," I said. "You guys don't have a clue how hard it is for an immigrant to come here and start with nothing."

I placed the bag on the little stainless shelf of the drive-up window.

"Please forgive us, brother. I'm sorry," I said sincerely. And I drove off.

After a ride of deep silence, the two Chicanos said, "You're right, we're sorry brother, we're sorry . . . that was cool what you did."

And the curandera and her prayers were real.

Suggestions for Teaching

In this story, students' understanding of one word will allow them to more deeply appreciate the events of the story. Although Jimmy explains the meaning of *curandera* in the second paragraph, for students with little or no background knowledge, it may not be enough. Help students conceptualize this word through the following activities.

Sample Lesson

1. Ask students to count the number of times Jimmy uses the word *curandera* and note where the word is used in the story.

2. In pairs, have students read the second paragraph of the story and discuss with each other their understanding of the term *curandera*. Determine students' background knowledge by asking if anyone has heard the word before and if so, in what context.

3. Explain to students how certain words, such as *war* or *love*, have many different meanings depending on the experiences of the person who is using the word. Set students on an inquiry journey—uncovering the layers that make up the word *curandera*. Students may opt to do one of the following:
   - Interview someone who has known a curandera or understands the term from his or her own culture.
   - Research the word online.
   - Write about someone they know who is like a curandera, based on their understanding of the term from Jimmy's story.

4. Have students share their knowledge of curanderas in small groups or with the whole class.

5. Then, have students read the story aloud, perhaps reader's theatre style, and discuss what Jimmy meant when he wrote, "And the curandera and her prayers were real."

Beyond the Classroom

Jimmy compares the curanderas he has met to "Frida Kahlo look-alikes." Have students find pictures of Kahlo and compare and contrast their own image of a curandera to photographs of Kahlo. Artistic students may take this activity further by drawing their vision of a curandera to post on classroom walls. Students may also enjoy reading the picture book *Frida* by Jonah Winter (2002) if they would like a visual experience of her art.

Forgiving the Godfather of Poetry

Lamont was a very cool cat, given a sweet gift of poetry. He was a Vietnam veteran, a community activist, and my friend. No better man. A young Afro-American ahead of his time surviving on the streets of Camden, New Jersey, he spent his time teaching the youngsters there how to love themselves.

The folks over at the Walt Whitman center invited me to come and read, and afterward Lamont walked me through the night streets of Camden, sharing with me the grisly statistics—number one in crime, severe poverty, lots of black-on-black violence, illiteracy, and despair.

I have to tell you, though, the people at the Walt Whitman center were amazing. They had a powerful organization, with community outreach employees who were meeting the challenges faceup in your grill—that is, they didn't theorize, they engaged; they didn't blackboard their ideas, they worked them out; they didn't armchair the youth to death with counseling, they walked beside them in the streets.

After the reading, we hung out to chat with the people and then I said good night, and Lamont walked me back to my room. We passed a lot of addicts, a lot of gangbangers. The streets were littered and the general unkempt and disheveled look of the place might have been a telltale sign of being ignored by the city counselors, but I knew if Lamont was any proof, a lot of artists lived in these run-down Victorian clapboards and creativity was thriving. He pointed to the county jail where I would be tomorrow, conducting a writing workshop, and we said good night.

It was a cold walk down to the jail from my hotel the next morning: frost on the windows, nasty old snow banked up on the streets' curbs, drug needles, snipped-off cocaine straws, liquor bottles, and beer cans wherever I glanced.

The jail, a five-story hulk of gray block with dark barred windows mirrored the winter's misery, its bitterness punishing the morning's hope with a dreamless despair.

Inside, my shoulder bag was checked, and I was patted down, walked through the metal detector, and swept with a wand by a guard. I collected my bag and coat and followed the guard upstairs and into a classroom that overlooked the gray streets below.

In a few minutes the cons came in, blacks and Latinos, mostly Puerto Ricans and Dominicans. This was a few years back and Mexicans hadn't flooded the east coast yet; now they are equal in number to the rest of the cons.

Once I had them in their seats, I paced back and forth in the front of the room and talked about the power of reading and writing. Most were fathers, all were drug abusers, many had been homeless and in a gang, almost all were in their twenties.

I treated them with great respect, keying in on topics to reference our similar experiences, trying to illuminate certain insights to help them endure the oppression they lived in daily.

I said, "Poetry is pretty much like fishing the outer banks of the mind. Writing is all about visiting those isolated islands in our hearts and learning how to make fire with rocks."

"Like sleeping on the sand in Santo Domingo and feeling the ocean waves channel deeper and deeper into your heart," a Dominicano cried.

"Exactly, my brother," I replied. "And then imagine that sacred water flushing out every impurity in your body and heart, and imagine every molecule in your body dancing with a sweet peacefulness you've never experienced before."

"Andale!" the Dominicano cried out again.

"Baile! Baile!" a Puerto Rican added.

They loved the magical aspects of poetry.

A tall Dominican was excited by the idea of writing a poem—he said, in a beautiful, warm, honeyed, coffee baritone voice, "I want you to help me write a poem to my wife—it's our anniversary today."

"Absolutely," I said. "We will all get the fires burning."

But no matter the hope I had offered, no matter how I had whittled down their heart's despair and elevated their esteem, all my words collapsed in crushing disappointment when I asked the guard to pass out pencils and paper so we could write poetry.

The guard said they were not allowed to have pencils, some sort of consequence for a recent situation wherein a convict was stabbed to death with one.

After trying to argue for pencils with the guard on duty, I resigned myself to a Q & A, telling the cons all sorts of stories about poetry: how Coleridge was an opium addict, Jack London a racist, Walt Whitman gay, and so on. I wanted to make these famous poets human to them, and they lit up with a thousand questions.

"What is a poem?"

"It's a sincere calling on spirits to visit you and bless you with words to express your darkest secrets and most radiant dreams."

"Can it be about bad stuff?"

"The most vile and corrupt acts humans commit, poetry turns into literary gems that reflect a truth that is in all of us."

Most of the men were engaged, but not the Dominican—his thoughtful visage was imbued with memories of his wife and the things they shared and did together. Eventually, he asked the guard for permission to use the bathroom and left.

We kept on talking about poets and poetry until the guard got suspicious of the Dominican being gone so long and he left the room to check on him.

That's when the alarm rang.

"Stay put in your chairs and don't move," the guard ordered the cons. "Over to the windows against the wall and stay put," he said to me.

I wondered if the Dominican tried to escape—or maybe hit a guard or something. Maybe he got into a fight with another con. I inhaled and walked around the room alongside the wall and then went out the door to the bathroom. A guard at the bathroom door said I was not allowed in, but when I looked, I saw what the Dominican had done.

They had already taken him down to the infirmary and were wiping the blood off the walls, blood he had scooped up with his fingers after cutting himself across the wrists. Blood he had painted on the wall composing the anniversary poem to his wife.

I left the jail and walked across the street to an apartment where Walt Whitman used to live and sat on the stoop of his house thinking that life can sometimes look real bleak.

What an irony, men forbidden to have pencils and paper in this place where the greatest American poet had lived a block away. In fact, when I'd been in the jail that morning, I could clearly see his house from the window in the classroom upstairs where we sat. I had been looking down on Walt's house when the alarm had sounded.

Looking down, I might add, feeling I was part of this cruel paradox. Here was Walt, a symbol of freedom and love and compassion and a block away, overlooking his house, was a jail that housed young men society had condemned to live without any of those humane principles.

I got up and walked a few blocks to the Camden cemetery where I found Walt's grave. Sitting next to it, I thought about how he believed in the doctrine of Manifest Destiny, that America was destined, even ordained by God, to expand across the entire continent. Many of my people, Native American Mexicans, indigenous Mexicans, tribal Mexicans with roots plunging deep into pre-Columbian times, were hanged, burned out, murdered, raped, and driven off their lands in the name of this doctrine. Manifest Destiny, soaked in my people's blood as it was, advocated this. Walt Whitman believed that God had blessed this slaughter, that America should extend coast to coast, from sea to shining sea.

I dug into my satchel and pulled out the eagle feather I carried everywhere with me and a half loaf of Indian fried bread. Placing both on his grave, I prayed. Sitting at his grave that day, I forgave Walt Whitman for his belief that had so dearly cost so many of my people.

Thirty minutes later I found myself walking into an elementary school. It was to be my last gig in Camden, and then I was going home.

The school looked more like a prison for kindergarteners. Coils of razor wire wrapped around the building, and at the entrance I had to insert my hand into a slot in the wall, place my palm flat on an ink pad, and press so a machine could read my fingerprints. While this was going on, a camera mounted high above clicked a snapshot of me. Someone manning a remote control board inside unlocked the latch and a voice came through a speaker, instructing me to enter.

The first thing that hit me overwhelmingly was the smell of fresh and warm oven-baked bread. It smelled so, so good and more so in contrast to the predatory streets and sorrowful experience of the Dominican convict.

A teacher escorted me to a classroom filled with thirty wide-eyed little African American angels and I asked my first question.

"How many of you know someone who has been hurt or killed by the drug dealers I saw standing on every corner this morning?"

Every kid raised a hand.

"Why then, if coming to school means you have to risk your life," I asked, "why do you come every morning? Especially when you know there's a possibility you may never reach the school?"

Every answer was the same—*because my momma wants me to get an education*.

So they risk their lives to get an education, I thought.

And because they were expected by all statistics and environmental laws to fail, and they weren't, I felt so delighted I was swept away on the wave of their determined innocence and I yelled out, "Come on! It's monkey pile time!"

I crouched on all fours in the center of the room and I was engulfed from all sides with giggling and screaming kids, each harboring a dream to be an artist, doctor, scientist, or carpenter, kids who refused to live in fear, reeking of cheap hair tonic and soap, with snotty noses and peed underpants, yet smelling as fragrant as any queen's garden in spring to my heart.

Suggestions for Teaching

Jimmy uses the term *cruel paradox* to explain his feelings about Walt Whitman's philosophy of life in contrast to the prisoners' reality. A careful reader will find other, less obvious paradoxes in this story as well. Help students better understand underlying meanings by having them reread the story carefully and with purpose. Use the following activity to generate dialogue.

Sample Lesson

1. Write the phrase *cruel paradox* on the board and ask students why Jimmy uses these words in the story. The word *paradox* can be difficult to understand, so take time to explore its meaning, pointing out that a *paradox* is something that seems contradictory but may expose a possible truth. Brainstorm with students paradoxes that may occur in life, such as being old enough to go to war at eighteen but not old enough to buy alcohol.

2. Ask students to read the story again, perhaps with a partner, and look for other paradoxes that are evident in the story, such as the prison-like atmosphere of the kindergarten, a poem written in blood, or children risking their lives to get an education in America.

3. Place students in small groups and ask them to discuss any paradoxes they may have found in the story after reading it more closely. Note that students may offer ironies or contrasts rather than true paradoxes, but accept all answers. The focus of this activity is to get students thinking about the events of the story in a deeper way.

4. Allow the groups to engage in a panel discussion. See Chapter 6 for more information on how to conduct this activity. Groups may use one or more of the following questions as a basis for their discussion:

   - What event or scene in the story is paradoxical, in your group's view?
   - Why is it a paradox?
   - What adjective would you use to describe the paradox? Use a word other than *cruel*.
   - What does such a paradox say about our society or our values?
   - How could this scene or event have been different?
   - How might a similar paradox affect you now or in the future?

Beyond the Classroom

In this story Jimmy refers to people and things that students may have heard about but which may not be a fixed part of their background knowledge, such as Coleridge, Jack London, Walt Whitman, and the Doctrine of Manifest Destiny. *Before* students read this story, offer extra credit to anyone who will research one of the above people or concepts and bring back information to the class. Have these students give a brief report to the class just prior to reading the story.

Sign Language, Convict Style

Prisoners all over the world, be it Korea, Russia, China, Mexico, or America, have created their own unique language to communicate with each other. In many prisons, convicts are not often allowed to speak, so over many decades they have learned to use their hands, facial features, and fingers to talk to each other from cell to cell, across cellblock landings, or from barred windows to their loved ones gathered on street corners, on the sidewalks of every downtown city in the world.

They must speak by signing in the convict code.

On the bed in my room, I spread out photographs taken by James Drake. He had express mailed me a batch of photographs saying he needed me to put poems to the photographs and he wanted me to hurry. The photos and the poems were going to be exhibited at the Whitney Museum in New York.

There were photos of prisoners signing through security Plexiglas to their loved ones in visiting rooms; photos of convicts signing through windows to acquaintances on street corners below; photos of prisoners signing to each other. As I studied photos of dolled-up girlfriends on street corners, I noticed rows of bail bond offices behind them.

The women were often pretty, the men tattooed and marked by hard street life. In many pictures, couples sat close to each other and signed through thick mesh wire embedded in bulletproof glass, their eyes reflecting the painful devastation of lovers caught in the blade-net of addiction.

© 2010 by Jimmy Santiago Baca, from *Adolescents on the Edge* by Jimmy Santiago Baca and ReLeah Cossett Lent. Portsmouth, NH: Heinemann.

I noted how their fingers bent to make letters, how both hands met midair or hip high to arrange a series of words that formed a sentence. The depth and breadth, width and height that this prisoner sign language embodied to articulate their misery and needs was startling. I could tell by the faces of the signer and responder that their conversation was deep, though it could be about anything from Grandma's latest recipe to their son's problems at school.

I felt sad for this fringe group of young people so on the margins of society that they had had to create their own sign language to communicate. At the same time, I was amazed by humanity's ingenuity to adapt to adverse circumstances.

The poems and the exhibit were a great success, but later, something even better happened. I had the opportunity to test the extent of the sign language and prove it was, indeed, a real language.

I had long heard Chino was the fiercest gladiator preparatory prison for young adults in the country, and I had been looking forward to this trip to the California State Youth Authority prison at Chino, not only because I wanted to try out the theory that had crystallized in my mind from the work I had done with James Drake, but because it was the perfect prison to see if my theory was right. We had a full week to test it and I was delighted.

My interns, Efren, Karina, Valentine, and I were met in the lobby by our host, a wonderful blonde-haired woman with an outgoing vitality in her speech and gestures. She had the kind of energy that made me want to take up running and swimming so I could exude the same aura of good healthy living. With her as our host, the workshop looked promising.

After passing through a series of weapon-detector gates where guards monitored the computer screens for guns or knives, another guard gave us a going-over with a contraband wand, and still another frisked and patted each of us down. Then we were led through several halls and out a door into the most welcoming broad compound flushed with bright daylight that ever warmed one's cheeks.

Here, a man with long graying hair and a turquoise necklace met us and introduced himself as one of the counselors at the prison. He was also the facilitator for the religious ceremonies of the natives in the prison. Everyone called him Uncle Jimmy.

As it turned out, over the next five days Uncle Jimmy would be extremely kind to us. He had a low-key disposition, and one would expect given the environment that he would be serious, but his conversation was lighthearted and his treatment of the inmates stern, but evenhanded.

Uncle Jimmy gave me free rein to roam about the library and mingle with the inmates. He let me arrange the seating of the inmates into groups, and he allowed me to assign my interns to various tables in the way I wanted.

On our first day in the classroom I explained to the convicts how I wanted them to write poems and recite them. After demonstrating several alternatives, I said I was also curious to know if they could sign and if so, could they translate a poem they wrote into sign language.

As I spoke, they sat still with immobile features. I knew they were appraising my every gesture, weighing every word, mulling over whether they should trust me with their life experiences. After all, words carry our feelings and pains and joys, and they had been violated by so many officials from the common policeman on the street to the judge to prison guards. Why reveal themselves to me? Why open themselves up?

I started out something like this:

"There's nothing I can say to win your trust, to make this writing workshop successful, to make it work for you. There's nothing I can say to lift you up from the silence you carry within and disarm you of your concerns enough to express your dreams and pains and loves.

"But you have to do it, trust me. I won't exploit you, I won't hurt you. I'll respect your experiences. And there is no such thing as too bad, too horrible a thing to write—express it, make it into a song we can all share.

"You have an obligation to do this, a responsibility to let all those young kids hustling on the street know that it is okay to express and share and write and read your heart out to others. Wail it, scream it, sing it, cry it, but get it out and let the world hear you.

"Teach me how to see you, how to know what your hands felt when they were crushed and broken under boots, teach me your loneliness when your father left you and your mother abandoned you, teach me how to understand you, to see the dark and the blood and the fear of your lives through your words, through poetry."

And they did.

When we were moved to the library the next day, we had more room to spread out and either Karina, Efren, or I could sit helping the inmates at each table. The whole time during the workshop we had two cameras filming, with the final cut to be aired nationally on *ABC World News Tonight with Peter Jennings*.

The guys got right into their work. I gave them a list of topics—love, hate, sadness, dreams, and so on and they plunged into each one with unabated eagerness. There was an urgency to their willingness to participate, and they were being open and trustful and cooperative.

Their questions were sincere.

"Mr. Baca, how do I write to my wife? How do I find the words to say what I mean? And especially to my little baby who I won't see for years?"

"Trust your words," I said. "Be simple, to the point. If you love, say 'I love.' Then put some details in—special times, special people, what the room looked like, the sky, the hour."

"Like, what if we just hung out on the corner, do we write about that?" another inmate asked.

"If the street corner was the center of your world, write about it. It's a lot more interesting than the darling worlds other writers write about. Aren't you a little tired of the darling books? Let's get real here. Going hungry is real, having no parents is real, being the target of racism and having no education is real; your life is filled with reality, sometimes sorrowful and sometimes happy, but real."

And that got them going. Hands sprang up with more questions.

"What about our guns or our crackhead fathers? Oh yeah, what about our dead homies?"

"Write about what you know. Great books are about what your lives are about. Problem is, you're letting others write about your lives. Don't you think it's time you step up and tell it like it is? Write about it. After all, you lived it. It's all about emotional truth, and *that* we need more of."

Then we performed.

One read a poem while another convict signed it. Another signed a poem to the class while the class wrote down what the signer was signing. It was unbelievable how extensive the language was. I had Crips signing to Bloods, the Mexican mafia signing to La Familia and the Border Brothers and the Texas Syndicato. Barriers disappeared. The space we worked in was hallowed and it gave no quarter to violence or hustlers.

And that was soon to be tested and proven.

We decided to have a public reading and all the participants in the workshop were pumped up to read before the inmates from outside the workshop. We took the liberty of inviting groups of convicts from several cellblocks to listen to our poetry.

I had a Crip stand twenty feet away from a guy in the Mexican mafia and this mafia guy twenty feet from a Blood and the Blood the same distance from another gangbanger. I wrote down a line of poetry and handed it to the first guy. He signed it and passed it to the next guy; the other signers sent it on, each signing the same sentence in their distinct gang dialect.

It was marvelous.

The very last gangbanger read it aloud. "Some-day-we-will-live-in-peace-and-all-get-along."

As that last convict finished speaking, out of nowhere and surprising everyone, a young black Crip in the audience started yelling about how gangbangers were not allowed to share signs with outsiders, how showing signs was prohibited. He cursed and threatened me until a Mexican warned him to be quiet and stop being disrespectful. He kept going until the guards removed him.

I wanted to tell the young man that was our problem—secrecy, holding things in, acting like secrets were our strength when our secrets were really weakening us.

On the way back to my hotel that day, I could still hear the black youth's voice and his fear in my head, "We can't be sharing our signs! They the enemy! They just want to get inside our code and then they'll use it against us."

It didn't matter if he was right or wrong. By not participating in a community exercise, he was depriving himself of communicating with others, isolating himself, denying himself this shared experience. Denying himself what allows us to be human.

The next morning he was found dead.

A Mexican came to the writing workshop that day stating he had to excuse himself from attending anymore. When I asked why, he said he loved the writing workshop so much he didn't want to bring bad energy into the room or corrupt the sanctity of the refuge for others.

"You see, Mr. Baca, when we share our feelings and dreams and pain, it's like sacred to me. I never got to do this, and it felt, like, it felt holy, you know. It made me feel like I was important, like I had some purpose. People were listening to me and I don't want to spoil that by bringing in bad energy for what I did."

"What bad energy?" I asked him.

He stared at me for a moment and then walked off.

And I understood what his eyes had told me.

Suggestions for Teaching

This is a story about language: words that "carry our feelings and pains and joys," sign language, body language, written language, and, finally, eyes that convey a tragic message. Perhaps your students have never thought about language as a conduit to their emotional lives or they may not even "trust words." Help them explore the power of language through the following activity.

Sample Lesson

1. Go back through the story and have students highlight or use sticky notes to identify the ways that Jimmy talks about language with the convicts, such as "trust your words" or "you're letting others write about your lives." Use the statements to generate a discussion about how people use words, give away their power of language, or withhold information, perhaps as a form of protection.

2. Read this passage from the story aloud to students: "Don't you think it's time you step up and tell it like it is? Write about it. After all, you lived it."

3. Tell students that for this writing session, they should feel safe to write whatever they please, whatever they may have been afraid to say, or whatever they wish they could communicate to someone.

Assure them that no one will read their papers, nor will the papers be graded, beyond a participation grade. Set the stage by insisting that everyone respect this process and each other by being totally quiet during the writing time.

4. At the end of fifteen to twenty minutes, tell students to reread their papers silently and make a decision about what to do with them. They may share their writing with the class or their writing partner, place it in their writing folders to revise at another time, give the piece to someone with whom they wish to communicate, turn the writing into a poem, or tear the paper into a hundred tiny pieces and throw them away.

Beyond the Classroom

This activity may melt writers' block forever for some students. Once they come to know the cathartic effect of such personal writing, many students become hooked. Make sure that each student has a personal writer's notebook, even if it is no more than a three-pronged folder with lined notebook paper. See Chapter 5 for a description of this writing tool. Then, encourage students to write outside of class, perhaps three times a week, experimenting with different forms, such as self-reflection pieces, poetry, observations, or letters. Provide time during class for sharing their writing. This practice will strengthen community, increase writing fluency, and give students space to use one of their greatest gifts: language.

The Embrace

On the last day of our stay at the Chino Correctional Facility, Uncle Jimmy threw a ceremonial sweat for us. We made our way to Uncle Jimmy's office, picked up a few sacred items and his medicine pouch, and then headed to the Native American Sweat Lodge, placed off in the corner on the main yard. It was surrounded with a high cyclone fence collared with coiled razor wire. A scruffy patch of gleaned brittle cornstalks befriended us in the way that an old summer garden gives of itself and then welcomes us back in a seasonal ritual of turning over the soil.

Inside the fenced enclosure, off to the side, were concrete showers where Valentine, Efren, and I changed into bathing suits Uncle Jimmy had given us. Then we walked across a little patch of parched grass into an area with leafless, gnarly elm trees lurched halfheartedly over a willow-branch-and-tarp sweat lodge.

About ten yards to the left and center of the sweat lodge, fifty or sixty convicts stood, naked except for the shorts they wore, stationed around the pit. Someone had started a big bonfire at the far end of the pit where dozens of volcanic rocks were reddening hot in the flames. The three of us slowly circled above on the rim, greeting each warrior encircling the pit.

There were many Chicanos with roots deep in Mexican tribes like Mechica, Nahuatl, Mayan, and Aztec. Each warrior handed each of us a gift—beaded bracelets, turquoise medallions, leather braided belts, and the like. They were beautiful, but even as my arms brimmed with heaps of gifts, I was stunned to see a blue-eyed, blonde-haired Indian. There were Asian and black Native Americans, too. I never knew they existed, but they did. They were standing before me.

After setting aside the gifts, we all entered the sweat lodge and Uncle Jimmy began the sweat by asking the Rock Carrier to bring in the rocks. He decided to start with twenty and when those rocks were in the sweat lodge, we began to sing our individual tribal songs. One by one each man stood in the darkness before the glowing red rocks and sang.

Each of the remaining men entered the sweat lodge until we formed a circle inside three deep. All sat, the first circle closest to the glowing rocks, enduring the excruciating heat, then the ones behind them in the second circle, and then the third bank of men against the tarp nearest the back.

When the last man had entered, Uncle Jimmy closed the tarp flap and all went dark, except for the glowing circle of rocks in the center.

A drum sounded, a rattle, and Uncle Jimmy's voice growled as if from the deep end of a faraway cave in Earth, uttering incantations that grew rounder and louder until it seemed we were all standing around the sun and hearing it slur out sweet rhyming vowels and growled consonants.

With each song came another hot volcanic rock until there were twenty-five, and then thirty. The whole time we sang and sang until all the rocks were brought in and the tarp flap closed permanently.

Uncle Jimmy sang and poured water over the red hot lava rocks. Then more water. More hot steam filled the dark confines. More song and more steam until my flesh felt like it were afire.

The hotter the lodge, the more we sang. Some men moaned and grumbled in agony; others writhed, trying to escape the scalding heat. Some wept aloud. Others yelped at the stinging pain. We all were experiencing the fragile flesh wrapped around our bones and heart. How vulnerable; how humbling.

And still Uncle Jimmy did not lessen the steam. During every song he scooped the ladle into the pail and refreshed the hot rocks, which sizzled with steam and made the men groan in agony.

Still hotter and hotter.

The steam represented the Creator's voice and presence, how the Creator manifested in the beginning when the universe consisted of numberless luminescent ribbons streaming in primordial infinity.

Steam was the Creator's breath. Steam was the way God spoke. Steam was the shape and form of our souls. Steam was the smoking mirror of the universe.

Valentine went on his belly behind me and started pawing the ground, gasping at the dirt, trying to suck oxygen from the soil. Efren curled up on his side behind me and endured the pain with clenched fists. I reached behind me in the dark and took each of their hands, and with their hands firmly in my grip, I sang louder and louder until my voice lofted above the others like a hawk looming, solitarily sailing on an updraft near the cliff's edge, its flight my song that drifted around the bodies of each man in the sweat lodge.

Uncle Jimmy then reached his tongs into the fire and grabbed a small red stone and pressed it against my back, bonding me to these men, now brothers, fusing me to this moment in time forever: a moment I would wear on my skin.

I gripped Val and Efren's hands tighter and sang, made the bonding go deep into the realm of soul bark, circle after circle to the core of deep bark, first year living bark, back-when bark, to the beginning of forest bark, and first hawk flight time.

But the best was yet to come.

No one was allowed to leave the ceremony, but one man started to wretch and heave and, begging forgiveness for breaking ritual, pled that he had to leave or die. When the flap opened and he left, I saw something that to this day still spreads a healing salve over my heart—as light came in from outside, my eyelids opened to see fifty convict-warriors surrounding me, embracing each other. I had never seen such a sight, men holding onto each other in the truest sense of what it means to love as men and affirming themselves as humans.

I had been looking for a cure for a long time, a cure that would heal myself, break through the brainwashing I had endured serving twenty-one years in the system—from orphanage, to detention home, to county jail, then on to Montessa Park for teenage gladiators, and finally to maximum-security prison. For more than two decades growing up, I had been taught to use my body as a weapon—that the flesh was a shield and a weapon to wound and scar and wield in battle.

This body, I learned, was not something in which one's heart thrived; nor was it a benign receptacle for feelings, or something a lover caressed. It was to be used to tolerate beatings, endure brutal afflictions, and then carried into the next wasteland arena of corrections abundant with hate, oppression, and institutional racism.

Eyes were to be crushed, mouths shattered, ears ripped off, tongues slashed, skulls crushed. We were taught this. To survive, one had to do it. Violence was the body's truest mate and bedfellow.

But for me, after leaving that life behind, I had a family, a wife and two sons, and I grieved privately that every time I went to hug my babies some horrible alarm went off in me and sounded the cruel alert that my body was not to enjoy a familial embrace—it was a warrior skin. For years and years I could not hug my children and feel calm and filled with love or feel that special warmth that comes with hugging one's children.

Until I saw these men in the sweat lodge hugging each other.

Their courage and sincerity healed me and moved me forward into another level of my own life. When I arrived back home after the sweat lodge and my sons picked me up at the airport in Albuquerque, it was the first time in my life that I hugged them and I didn't feel ashamed or awkward.

I felt loved, with the capacity to love in return.

Suggestions for Teaching

In the sweat lodge, Jimmy undergoes a change, "a cure," through an almost surrealistic bonding he experiences with others. The events in this story are so powerful that students will need time to talk with one another and explore their feelings about what they have read. Allow them to respond with a partner or in a small group. Then, help students understand the change Jimmy describes by making a connection to their own lives. Use the following activity to help them process and internalize this riveting story.

Sample Lesson

1. Have students read the following sentence aloud to a partner (and the partner will read it back again to the first student) and then discuss any thoughts they may have about what Jimmy's voice symbolizes in this story: "My voice lofted above the others like a hawk

looming, solitarily sailing on an updraft near the cliff's edge, its flight my song that drifted around the bodies of each man in the sweat lodge."

2. Have students read the following paragraph in the same way (out loud to each other) and discuss the meaning of "warrior skin": "But for me, after leaving that life behind, I had a family, a wife and two sons, and I grieved privately that every time I went to hug my babies some horrible alarm went off in me and sounded the cruel alert that my body was not to enjoy a familial embrace—it was a warrior skin. For years and years I could not hug my children and feel calm and filled with love or feel that special warmth that comes with hugging one's children."

3. Tell students to think about their own voices and skins. Encourage them to think metaphorically, reminding them of how Jimmy used the terms to show his reader something about himself.

4. Tell students they may choose to write either about their voice or their skin—or they may do both if they like. Provide the following stems and ask students to complete them, trying to use metaphor in the way Jimmy did.

When I was born, my voice . . .

When I was born, my skin . . .

When I was a child, my voice . . .

When I was a child, my skin . . .

As a teenager, my voice . . .

As a teenager, my skin . . .

When _____ happened, my voice . . .

When _____ happened, my skin . . .

Today, my voice . . .

Today, my skin . . .

Tomorrow, my voice will be . . .

Tomorrow, my skin will be . . .

5. Students may turn their writing into poems or memoir pieces—or they may place them in their writing portfolios for later revision.

Beyond the Classroom

Tell students about the deaths of two people in a sweat lodge in Arizona, October 2009, under suspicious circumstances (http://edition.cnn.com/2009/US/10/15/arizona.sweat.lodge/index.html). Ask students to research traditional uses of sweat lodges, as Jimmy describes in his story, as well as the online account of what happened in Arizona. They may use their research as the basis of a class discussion about the safety and sanctity of sweat lodges.

Birdhouses

I was truthful in what I had just said to the group of women I'd been working with in the Grants Prison, located in Grants, New Mexico, but stunned by the question that followed.

For three months I had been bringing a documentary crew to film our writing workshop and every week, as the women trusted me more and more, they disclosed the horrors of how men had treated them. No—I should change that word, from *horrors* to *torture*.

And I couldn't take it anymore.

So I told them, "Look, no more stories about men burning you, beating you, about fathers and uncles and mother's dates raping you, no more blood and cuts and overdoses, and bleak and horrible events and incidents. Let's write a bit about more happier things."

But they had none.

That's when the woman asked, "If we can't write about our families, then what the hell do we do? You're the teacher. We can't just make shit up."

For a couple of weeks I thought about what she had said and then I came up with a solution.

I didn't know if I would be permitted to do it but I was going to try anyway. So I drove down to Santa Fe, to the offices of Cabinet Secretary of Corrections, Joe. He was a good guy, from the South Valley where I was from, and he had given me plenty of leeway to do my documentary project.

But when I asked him to be allowed to bring birdhouses in to the women, and also to be allowed to paint them together and set them around the prison, he balked.

"What the hell you trying to pull?" he said.

When I explained my reasons and plan to him, he cautiously and begrudgingly agreed.

"But if anything goes wrong," he warned, "it's the end of the writing project."

The following week when I met the women and told them I was bringing in birdhouses, they seemed elated. I didn't tell them what my plan was, just that we were going to be doing some serious writing, and serious didn't mean somber and tragic, but celebratory.

I've always kept my word and this was no different, just a little harder. The day of the workshop, the guards had to check out not only the camera equipment and such but the birdhouses and paints, and when I walked in, I was a little bit late. Not that late, but it didn't stop the women from scolding me—until I told them I had a surprise.

"Remember I told you I couldn't take the grief any more? No more asshole men making you hold drugs, punk-gangsters busting you and your kids . . . no more?

"Well, come on up here and pick out your birdhouse. You're about to have new families."

I had no idea how powerful this was going to be. The women took the birdhouses and started painting them according to their cultural ethnicity. African American women painted their houses African style—yellows, blacks, reds, tribal symbols. The Chicanas did their houses in Mexican colors—green, yellow, red, and loaded the walls with murals from their tribal affiliations: Mechica, Mayan, Incan, etc. The Caucasians followed with Appalachian and medieval colors and motifs.

The one thing they had in common was that they all wept and wept as they painted their birdhouses. I mean really wept. Tears poured down their cheeks and streamed into the paint, discoloring the original pigment with salty tears of passionate forgiveness.

They were feeling in themselves their primal innocence again, experiencing early dreams they hadn't allowed themselves to remember because the pain of betrayal had shattered their childhood hopes.

This ritual of creating a new beginning was their personal baptism, cleansing them of their previous sorrows and reinvigorating their faith in the goodness of themselves.

The next week we set up the birdhouses outside the prison building but inside the fenced perimeter. We agreed that whatever birds arrived at their birdhouses, this was going to be their newly adopted family. For weeks after that, the women monitored their specific birdhouse and soon their journals filled up, page after page. It was impossible to keep them from writing.

The women acted like expectant mothers, chattering about their new child, about a new father, about the wonderful bird mother. Hawks, blackbirds, sparrows, owls, and other birds appeared at the birdhouses and I had a lively flock on my hands.

The women became effusive and enthusiastic and were impossible to contain. They laughed about their children, about the habits of their bird mothers, how cute and lovely they were, and so on. The women learned about nature writing, about describing the sky and the Earth, but in a very real and connected way. They reconnected to childhood feelings and embraced the sparrow as if it were an angelic messenger with a specific tiding to enrich their hearts with joy.

Then one day, while reading to the women good examples of descriptive nature writing by John Muir, Edward Abbey, and another page from Turgenev on landscape, Lonnie rushed up and declared with alarm, "Maria's in trouble."

I ran to her "home" and found her kneeling on both knees cradling a bloody but very dead sparrow. A red-tailed hawk a few houses down had killed it.

There was very little we could do to console her—dead is dead. It's a facet of life we learn to accept since we cannot avoid it. Maria and some women dug a hole under the birdhouse and buried the bird and prayed over it, wishing it a good journey into the beyond. Maria and a couple of her friends walked back to the classroom and I stayed with the other women outside.

We talked about unforeseen accidents and our responses to them. How we deal with death, how we have to relearn how to grieve, how we have to embrace the community in our grief, publicly admit our loss, be unashamed to let others view us in our darkest hours.

We talked about how not to hide our loss, mask it in pretty clothes and nice cars, subdue it with drugs, numb or cauterize it with blatant bravura as if the tragedy didn't happen to us, as if it didn't affect us at our deepest core. And right in the middle of this discussion, while I was using St. Francis' life as an example, a woman cried my name out from the education building.

"Jimmy!" she hollered, waving me toward her. "Maria's lost it."

I flew toward the building and as I entered the classroom, I saw Maria hurling a chair against the wall. I also heard guards coming down the hall and when they were just about to plunge into the room wielding clubs, I begged the captain to please let me calm her down.

The captain motioned the guards back and I began to talk to her softly.

"Maria, death jolts us into a frailty that allows us to glimpse our beauty. Loving through sorrow is a great gift—it's a powerful incentive to love those who are alive. Death allows us to renew our efforts to appreciate life. It's through our sorrow we become known to ourselves."

Though it sounded like unapproachable philosophy, she understood my words and the emotion behind them.

Maria and I sat together for a good thirty minutes, with the rest of the women in the background, slowly inching their way forward until they surrounded us and we all crowded in and held each other in a communal show of trust and empathy.

Shortly after this incident, the State of New Mexico contracted the Corrections Corporation of America to take over and administer the prison. Their first move was to destroy all the birdhouses.

Suggestions for Teaching

This story offers an opportunity to help students understand how symbols work in narration and how powerful they are in defining our beliefs and values. Explain the meaning of the word *symbol* and, in small groups or with a partner, have students come up with symbols that are a part of their lives, from the ubiquitous McDonald's golden arches to name-brand clothes, symbols we wear that make a statement about what we believe or who we are. Then, read the following sentence to students: "This ritual of creating a new beginning was their personal baptism, cleansing them of their previous sorrows and reinvigorating their faith in the goodness of themselves." Ask students how the ritual of creating birdhouses became symbolic of a new life for these women.

Sample Lesson

1. Have students read the story a second time with a specific purpose. Using a highlighter or sticky notes, ask them to mark any symbols that they see in the story and be ready to explain what they symbolize. Point out that colors can be symbols as well.

2. Allow students to share the symbols they found with a partner and then with the whole class. If students don't mention them, make sure they understand that the birdhouses may symbolize home and the sparrow may symbolize family. Ask why these symbols were so important to these women.

3. Encourage students to make connections from the story to their own lives. For example, if students have cars, they may see them as their homes, they may view a particular teacher as a mother or father figure, or they may feel that a certain color symbolizes joy, despair, or good times. They may wish to list these on paper and put them in their writing folder, to use as the basis for a poem or piece of writing.

4. Then, provide students with blank paper and markers, crayons, or colored pencils. Tell students to create a design that they would put on their own "birdhouse," one that signifies in some way something important to them. It could be a design from their tribal affiliation, culture, or ethnicity, as the women in the story used, or a color, a graphic, or a unique design that students create.

5. Display the designs on the wall and ask each student to make a brief presentation about what their design means. Encourage them to pair music with their design for a sensory experience.

Beyond the Classroom

In this story, Jimmy said the women learned about nature writing. Ask students what this might mean and then tell them to discover nature writing on their own. They should take their writer's notebooks and find a place in nature (even in a park or under a tree), close their eyes, and just be aware of what they are experiencing—a squirrel rustling the leaves or a cool breeze raising goose bumps on their arms. Then, they should open their eyes and really see what is around them. Finally, they should freewrite, exploring how writing deepens this experience. Students may want to share their papers with others in the class or you may turn this into a class literary magazine complete with nature poetry, observations, drawings, and photographs.

The Warden

I was invited to come to Phoenix, Arizona, to give a keynote speech at a conference on prison reform. It was a national conference, attended not only by correction reformers but wardens, cabinet-level secretaries of corrections from different states, security staff, and educators in the secure setting areas.

A woman from the Justice Department informed me she was bringing a new study on prison reform—statistics, new methodology, alternative punishments, community engagements. I was intrigued, but when I arrived she met me in the lobby and handed me this four-inch-thick collection of data to read.

"I believe you will be very interested in the direction corrections is going. We're developing some very unique approaches to rehabilitation," she said.

It had never crossed my mind that I'd have to set aside months to read the study. For me, prison reform was pretty cut and dried—you cannot rehabilitate anyone without community involvement and education. I took the huge tome to my room, threw it in my suitcase, and promised myself I'd skim it over for essentials in the coming months.

I got ready to give my keynote for the conference and later that afternoon took my seat at a table for lunch in the conference hall. There were about five hundred people there, all excited about sharing and networking and renewing old contacts and making new ones.

Before I was called up, the emcee gave recognition to those hard workers who had made the conference possible and then he announced they had a special guest in the audience. It was a warden, who was being honored with a gold watch for fifty years of dedication in performing his duty as a warden at several prisons.

I looked at the old man hobbling up to the stage and thought I recognized him. Perhaps no. I knew many wardens from the many prisons where I had given innumerable writing workshops since my release.

I walked up to the retired warden and gave him a free stack of my signed books. He shook my hand with genuine gratitude, and I slapped his back in a friendly fashion, offering congratulations. I then went up to the stage and proceeded to speak about prison reform, what I believe works and doesn't work.

"If you dehumanize a person in action and environment," I began, "words to humanize him will never work. If you send a man to school in the day and allow him to get gang-raped at night, what good is the education when the man has lost his will to live? If you reward a bully with extra desserts at dinnertime because he beat someone up, and mock the man who refuses to fight, you spread the venom of unconscionable violence into our culture and society and promote it as a way to live. If you design a place that praises what is evil, then expect evil acts. This is what prison does, has done, and will always do.

"Prison is as traumatizing as war, as life destroying as addiction, as community breaking and family destroying as a killer on the loose. Except that the killer will one day be free and enter your home, abduct your child, addict your loved ones, terrorize your peaceful life, and take the life of innocents.

"We must confront this social scourge called crime, and deal with criminals in a way that they will stop committing crime. We must change it, and to do that we need the community involved."

In the middle of the crowd, the retired warden sat with his gold watch, about twenty tables deep, right in my line of sight. And as I spoke, who he was and where I knew him from hit me with the force of a lightning strike.

He was my warden.

But not only was he my warden. He was the one who had me escorted to his office, the one who had hit me and vowed *on my death* that I would work or die.

I could still hear his voice. "*No one* in my prison gets away with not working," he'd said. "I'll bury you out back in an unmarked grave if you don't work."

Did he remember the afternoon years ago when he charged from around his desk, pit bull–stout, looming over me, huffing with rage? From the side of my left eye, I'd seen a blur, and a second later his fist had smashed into my cheek.

This was the man who had sent vicious inmates down to my isolated cell to fight me. This was the warden who had sent goons down to my dungeon cell to beat me.

And why?

Because I wanted to attend GED classes and he said I couldn't. He ordered me to work; I refused. And because I refused, this warden kept me locked up in isolation month after month. For the remaining time I spent in prison, I was never permitted to attend school and I continued to refuse to work.

And Lord have mercy, how The Creator works in mysterious ways indeed—some fifteen years later, he was sitting right before me.

I did not know if I should tell him who I was or not. Was it not enough that I should have a dozen books published and be in such demand as a speaker that my calendar for each year filled within weeks? Was it not enough that I was now a poet using my life to free and heal spirits and write poems? Had life not already rewarded me a million times over with an abundance of poems, friends, family, and fame, while he had spent his time locking people up—had in a very concrete sense spent his life locked up by his own choice and willingness?

You could see it in his craggy and wrinkled face, in his eyes that had lost their light. His soul's death reeked with the stench of a rotting carcass. He sat intently listening to my words when I simply couldn't restrain myself any longer from sharing what I knew with the crowd.

Directing my voice and eyes to the warden, I spoke. "Do you know who I am? Do you remember me?"

He squinted and pinched his brows together, shuffled through his old finger-worn deck of memory cards and shook his head no.

"I'm Jimmy Santiago Baca. I was in your prison at Florence for six years, and you vowed I'd never see daylight unless I obeyed you and went to work."

He seemed confused.

"Seventy-two to '78. You had me put in the dungeon for years. I remember you brought me to your office one day and because I had a red ink pen in my pocket you badgered me about loving blood, and had the guard, what was his name . . . oh yeah, Five Hundred, hit me from behind while I sat in the chair looking at you."

He got it. His face turned red and he stood and swept the books off his table. Then he walked out.

At that moment I realized how good it felt to have someone *else* have to walk out of a room. For many years I was the one walking out, and now it was the warden who walked out and I who stayed to finish my speech.

All my life, from classrooms where the nuns told me to leave for misbehaving, to wanting to say something and being hushed or ignored, to being a no one, unknown and unimportant, to being chased off my indigenous lands, forbidden to speak my language or practice my rituals in public—always, I'd been chased off and ordered to leave.

And now he had to leave the room and I stood tall and empowered and spoke from my heart.

Life deals you a beautiful hand to play from time to time.

Suggestions for Teaching

While students will instantly appreciate the irony with which this story ends, there is more that they can ponder. The topic offers students an opportunity to think critically about what they believe regarding prisons, criminals, and the role of the community in dealing with crime. But students should make informed evaluations, and that means taking the time to become knowledgeable about a topic. Take students through the following activity in preparation for a class forum about prison reform. See Chapter 6 for more information about forums.

Sample Lesson

1. Begin by having the students read the story again in groups of four, with one student each taking the following parts: narrator, warden,

the woman from the corrections department, and Jimmy (as he speaks). When all groups are finished, have them return to Jimmy's speech, beginning with the line, "If you dehumanize a person. . . ."

2. Ask students to write a response in their journals to what Jimmy said. Tell them that such freewriting is necessary to get them thinking about what they believe in regard to the treatment of criminals.

3. When students finish writing, engage them in a whole-class discussion, using some of the following questions as a basis for discussion:
   - What does it mean to "dehumanize a person"?
   - How should criminals be treated in prison?
   - Should different types of criminals be dealt with differently, such as those who commit violent crimes versus those who are drug dealers or users? Explain.
   - Why do you think Jimmy believes that prisons are as traumatic as war or addiction?
   - How can our society "deal with criminals in a way that they will stop committing crime"?
   - What is a good prison?
   - What role does the community have in creating good prisons?

4. After the discussion, have students jot down one idea from the discussion that they would like to pursue in more depth.

5. Help students translate their "idea" into a research topic or essential question.

6. Give students time in the library or in the computer lab to research their topic. Also, if possible, arrange for them to interview people who might have information to share on the topic, such as correctional officials, someone who has been in prison, or relatives of prisoners. See Chapter 6 for information on conducting interviews.

7. Students should use the information to form their own "solution" to the problem they are researching.

8. Have each student (or team) present their findings in the following format:
   - What is the essential question (or research topic)?
   - What did the research show?
   - What solution do they offer?

9. If time permits, students may wish to put their ideas together in a booklet or create a wiki blog as a way of continuing the dialogue.

Beyond the Classroom

Consider giving students firsthand knowledge of how jails or prisons operate as well as how prisoners are treated by arranging to have students tour a local correctional facility. They should take their writer's notebooks so they can jot observations that might be useful in their class presentations.

Saving the Tree

I admit it might have looked like a dumb move on my part if you value only money, as many people do, but sometimes enough stupid moves pile up to make a tidy little karmic stash—and even a few happy days.

It started when I was in the market for a house. Well, before that. It began when I arrived home one night from reading poetry and found my house on fire. Dozens of boxes of journals and writings, first drafts of poetry books, scores of characters and events and experiences I had written about, all with the hopes of one day spending serious time maturing the kernels into good poems, were now on the floor smoking in the ashes.

Yes, it was terrible. But in a sense it was also a relief.

For a long time, I had wanted to carry my notebooks to the trash and throw them away, but I feared I'd be tossing out work that might be good. I'd been harboring my early writings out of insecurity and when they burned, a weight lifted from my shoulders, freeing me with courage to start new work.

That night as I rummaged through the debris, hoping to salvage family photos, a neighbor of mine came over, a gangbanger named Chris, and handed me some cocaine, tequila, and a joint. I thanked him, but declined. Walking through the charred house, bidding good-bye to my past, I felt secretly refreshed the fire had taken the old writing away.

Shortly after that I was riding the back farm roads of Los Padillas when I found an old, crumbling adobe house with the biggest American elm tree I had ever seen standing nearby.

I fell in love with that tree.

In fact, I parked my car in the tall, weedy driveway and checked to see if the farm gates were open. They were locked, so that afternoon I slept in my car listening to the huge branches of the elm sway lightly in the breeze and feeling the immense loving and compassionate presence of this grandmother tree.

When I woke and asked the neighbors who owned the house and land, they told me "a crazy woman." They pointed to a two-story house at the end of the dirt road, surrounded with handsome fields heavy with green alfalfa.

They said that the house was falling down and uninhabitable, that the floor and walls were caved in and infested with mice and field rodents. There were even weeds growing up through the floorboards.

Nonetheless, the next day, I parked at the gate again, walked down the dirt road to her house, and pushed the red button on her cyclone fence gate topped with barbwire. Into the intercom, I stated my name and reason for wanting to talk to her. The gate slid back on wheels, and I went up the steps. She greeted me at the door.

She was rich. She owned many acres all around, including the decrepit adobe a few fields away. Thin and haggard with a cavernous face, heavy jaw, and scrawny voice, her eyes peered rather than looked. As kids, my friends and I would have called her a witch.

I told her I wanted to buy the house next door and even she admitted only a dunce would want to buy it. She was intending to destroy the house, hire a dozer, and raze it.

"That nasty tree," she spit out, "I'm going to chop it up into stove pieces and burn it this winter."

Being rich, I guessed, the tree was an economic problem for her— its roots would one day fracture the foundation of her house, or the branches would crash on the roof one windy night and cost her money she wasn't willing to spend. For me, it was a beautiful gift from the Earth.

I told her I had a little money, not much, and I was anxious to ask her the price. When she said $90,000, I had to breathe in with effort to keep my composure. It was way more than I could afford. My only hope was to come back and see her and beg her to lower the price.

When I told the neighbors the price she quoted me, they laughed.

"You're not foolish enough to pay that are you?"

I was. I had my heart set on it.

Many gasped, wide-eyed and open-mouthed, shaking their heads, certain I was insane. "It's all falling down, how you going to live there? You're going to spend more money fixing it up than you will paying for it."

Still others used the rich lady's quote as evidence of her mental incapacity. "That just proves my point—she's plumb nuts."

I was still going to buy it. Not for the house, but to keep the tree from being cut down. I would find the money somehow.

While my brother and I worked to rebuild my burnt house with the insurance money, I couldn't get the tree out of my mind. It kept calling to me, entering my dreams, penetrating my thoughts each day. In fact, I went down there daily and looked at the tree. One day I climbed over the fence and stood next to it and embraced it. Embraced a part of it, that is, since it would have taken six adults holding hands with arms extended horizontally to encircle it.

Hugging it, I could feel the energy in the bark that sizzled in every inch. I could feel its massive roots below me, going down perhaps hundreds of feet; there were movements in the roots, a presence like breathing in the dark. Most of all, I felt the tree look down on me from its towering height and bless me, acknowledging my affection for it.

With each of my visits, this feeling that the tree was alive and sensitive to my love intensified, becoming stronger and stronger even in my dreams.

I believe in things that have no foundation or basis to believe in and likewise with the house. I was out in the yard carrying lumber and just about done rebuilding my house that burned down. My brother was a carpenter by trade and a good one, and out of the ashes of the old house, he had constructed a beautiful new little home. We were both admiring our work when a stranger drove up and asked if I was selling it. I asked him for a price he thought was fair. He gave it and I accepted. Life is strange; sometimes it brings you just what you need.

Within a month I was moving into the adobe house. And many an evening I sat on the porch and reflected on the tree and me. We had something between us—a joy, a somber grace, an understanding.

That elm tree became my symbol of strength, a symbol of endurance, a reminder of how the rich lady had wanted to cut it down as so many people in my life had wanted to cut *me* down.

Yet both of us had survived.

In some way we both understood that. We were two friends trying to restore our hope, live with dignity, and for me, trying to heal the lightning-strike wound of being homeless, both believing the sun would rise at dawn and we'd have another chance to grow.

Suggestions for Teaching

While students may agree with Jimmy's friends, that he was crazy for spending all that money to save a tree, they may also understand his desire to go to any lengths to save something that was important to him, especially something he considered to be a friend. Help students find their own "tree" through the following activity.

Sample Lesson

1. Begin by asking students in what way Jimmy and the tree are alike. They will look at the last few paragraphs of the story to answer this question, but push them to find other similarities that aren't stated explicitly in the story, such as "They both had been abandoned," or "They both had deep roots."

2. Ask students to think about one of their friends and list ways that they and that particular friend are alike. Again, encourage them to go beyond the obvious like "We have the same color hair," or "We both like pizza," and consider, for example, how their goals for the future or their past experiences are similar.

3. Next, have students write about their relationship with their friend, using a jot list as prewriting. Following are some prompts for students:
   - a time you came to each other's rescue
   - a time you did something for your friend (or he or she did something for you) that others thought was crazy

- why your friend is so much like you
- how you see your friendship developing in a year, five years, twenty years
- what your friendship symbolizes
- how others see your friendship

4. Use this familiar piece of writing to take your students through the writing process. See Chapter 5 for more information on revision and editing.

Beyond the Classroom

Have students ask their parents or other adults close to them about a friend they remember as being a soul mate. The next day, ask students to share their findings with the class or a small group before continuing to write about their own friend.

Interview with
Jimmy Santiago Baca

From Chicano down-and-out street tough and maximum-security-prison denizen to poetry slam champion, holder of the Wallace Stevens Chair at Yale, and recent winner of Germany's most prestigious International Award, Jimmy Santiago Baca has led a most unusual life. Filled to the brim with great pleasures and sufferings, harmonies and contradictions, his breathtaking poetry, fervent memoir, sharp-sighted short stories, social dramas, and other creative work are a testimony to this and form an important cornerstone to Chicano/a and American letters today.

Born in 1952 in New Mexico to a Chicana mother and an Apache Indian father, Baca learned swiftly and suddenly the pains of not belonging. After his father died of alcoholism and his mother packed her bags for California, the young Baca found himself first living with his grandparents and then deposited in an orphanage. After years of growing up within the walls of the orphanage and dropping out of high school, Baca hit the streets of Albuquerque to find solace with other like-minded, deeply alienated Chicanos. Barely getting by and treading deep the streets of cities scattered throughout the Southwest, in 1973 he found himself charged with possession and intent to distribute drugs, and was sentenced to a six-year lockup in a maximum-security prison in Florence, Arizona.

Four years of isolation plus electric shock treatment did not break Baca's spirit. Indeed, Baca turned his internment into a self-fashioned chrysalis: starting from scratch, he first learned how to read and write; subsequently he applied himself to master words and aesthetic forms, and ultimately he devoted himself to become a creator with both. All along this unusual apprenticeship he never lost sight of his one and only goal: to use the power of literature to build new worlds, new meanings, new emotions, and new interpretations in order to help his readers reach a position from which the actual world could be perceived under a different light.

With a GED tucked safely under his arm, Baca walked out of prison ready to face the world as a self-identified Chicano poet. Baca's *pinta* (prison) poetry resonated loudly with audiences inside and outside of the state penitentiary. While still in prison, his first poems saw the light of day in *Mother Jones*, and a year before his release he published his first chapbook, *Jimmy Santiago Baca* (1978). In these early poems, his already exceptional lyrical voice speaks out against the dehumanizing conditions of prison life. The year of Baca's release from the penitentiary in 1979 also marked the publication of his first collection of poetry, *Immigrants in Our Own Land and Selected Early Poems*.

In between working as night watchman, janitor, laborer, and numerous other jobs, Baca had to fight against his own demons (drug addiction and alcoholism) and to find inside himself the resources to continue writing. A new chapbook of his appeared, *Swords of Darkness* (edited by Chicano author Gary Soto), and then a second book, entitled *What's Happening?* (1982). Baca was promptly becoming recognized as one of the great new Chicano poets, albeit a controversial one.

In 1987, Baca published *Martin and Meditations on the South Valley*, a semiautobiographical poem about the epic journey of the orphaned Martin across "countless towns" in America and the eventual finding of roots in family and home. *Martin* won the American Book Award, and in 1989 it was followed by the publication of the *Black Mesa Poems*, in which Baca continues to portray the rich lives of Chicanos and Chicanas.

While Baca is mostly known for his poetry, he has also availed himself outstandingly of other means of expression: in 1991 he brought out a play, entitled *Los tres hijos de Julia*; in 1993 he wrote a screenplay entitled *Bound by Honor/Blood in Blood Out*; and more recently he published a collection of gritty realistic and magical short stories, *The Importance of a Piece of Paper* (2004), and a novel, *A Piece of Glass* (2009). In his memoir, *A Place to Stand* (2001), he tells in lyrical prose the story of his life. Baca continues to write in Albuquerque. He also works with at-risk youth and convicts nationwide through his nonprofit, Cedar Tree, Inc.

Early Life

Q: You have had a pretty rough life. Let me just run through with you some of the things that have happened to you. You were born of both Chicano and Apache descent. Your parents divorced and abandoned you when you were 5 years old. Why did they abandon you?

JSB: I guess the reason they abandoned me was that they didn't know how to take care of themselves. They were being assaulted and assailed from all sides. Well, you know, when that happens, how can you cope with taking care of kids when you can't even take care of yourself?

Q: How did you end up in an orphanage?

JSB: I was taken there because the authorities thought it was bad influence to be around the people of my Pueblo. They thought that I should learn how to speak English and be a Catholic.

Q: So you left the orphanage when you were twelve? Did you run away, or did they release you?

JSB: Well, I ran away a lot of times. I had this problem, as Nerudas says in one of his poems, I had "little tiny flames" shooting out from my heels . . . as most children do. They were going to send me to Boys Town, and I ran away. Ultimately, I just never came back.

Q: Where did you live? How did you live?

JSB: Well, you know, I hustled. . . . I really depended on the kindness and the generosity of my people. And I lived with many friends and families. They would give me a meal and they would give me food. The hardest part about living on the streets as a kid is when the rest of the kids are in school, and the grown-up adults have gone to work, and you are left with the very ancient, or the handicapped, or the invalids, you begin to think there must be something wrong with you, too, that you're one of the damaged ones.

Q: Did the chaos of your childhood teach you how to risk?

JSB: Yes. At almost every turn in the road, I had to face my fear. "What will be this person's response if I confront them? If I admit I don't know something? If I show how scared I am?" There's an organic order in the chaos around us that you have to find. It's in the apparent chaos of nature, this order. Poetry helps me find that order in myself and then everywhere around me. I find order in the saddest sorrow.

Prison Life

Q: How did you end up in prison? What were the charges?

JSB: Drugs, possession, with intent to sell, to distribute.

Q: Once you were in prison, did you have any goals or were you just trying to do your time and get out?

JSB: I wanted to go to school and the counselor promised I could go to school if I didn't get in trouble, so I worked 60 days in the kitchen, getting there at four in the morning. It was a beautiful experience to go out that time of morning. I'd stand in the yard until the guard came and got me. I would look at the moon and smell the desert smells. It affected my soul in a big way. My dream was to go to school and learn how to read and write and then go back to villages and work with kids.

Q: So, did you get to go to school?

JSB: They reneged on the deal and betrayed me, said I couldn't go to school. When that happened, something broke down in me in the reclassification committee meeting. They said, "You're going out in the field." I couldn't get out of the chair. I remembered being hit by this guard named 500. The last thing I saw was the room whirling. He had hit me so hard that I had flown out of my chair.

Q: Why did they call him 500?

JSB: He was over 500 lbs. He broke all the ribs on my left side. He broke my jaw. They had to wire my jaw back together. Any type of defiant behavior like that has to be dealt with immediately. Here was a convict who was saying he wanted to go to school and for some reason the committee thought that was more dangerous than stabbing somebody.

Q: What did you do?

JSB: I went to my cell and refused to work, and the repercussions of that one decision sent off a frenzied current of confusion, not only through the homeboys I was in a gang with, but the guards freaked out too. The warden came down and said, "If you don't start getting in line, you're not going to walk out of here."

Q: What happened then?

JSB: They sent Mad Dog Madrill. He was the one person you did *not* want to visit you.

Q: He was a guard or a prisoner?

JSB: A guard.

Q: What happened when this brutal guard came in?

JSB: He pulled me out of my cell and took me to isolation. As I was standing on the landing and watching them tear my cell apart, other convicts all started throwing stuff at me. I tried to disassociate myself from myself and say this is not really me. Someone threw hot water, and someone threw urine, and someone threw feces at me. It's even hard to talk about. I wiped it off. I turned around and I kept saying to myself, "They're not mad at me; they're mad at somebody else." All of a sudden the guards came and chained me up and walked me out of the cell block. I'll never forget this feeling when I walked out; I was suddenly filled with an overwhelming sense that I had wanted to do this since I was born. I just wanted to make a choice in life, whether it was right or wrong. It gave me this overwhelming peace or purpose. It was like I had a role in life.

Q: How did you survive? Did they put you in the hole? Did they brutalize you?

JSB: For three years they knocked the living hell out of me. They broke a lot of bones and I became somewhat of a hero because I lived in administrative custody where they called me a security risk. The guards would come down and beat me, but I would fight them and then wake up in isolation.

Q: What did you do down there during the long days?

JSB: I was reading so many things. I was not really in prison; I was some place else. They had left me alone by this time and they had put me with the death row inmates. It's great to be near the death row inmates because they read the really great books, not comic books, you know? They are preparing for the next world.

Q: They didn't want to waste their time?

JSB: No, they didn't want to waste their time. I was reading *For Whom the Bell Tolls*, Fitzgerald's *Great Gatsby*. I asked myself, "Who kept this from me? Why didn't they give this to me? Why did I stray off and float like flotsam along the beach? I have a right to read; this is my legacy as an American." So I was reading voraciously.

Q: Did you begin to write then?

JSB: Well, the first poem I wrote I stole out of the Bible. I replaced the words so I could send a poem to a woman I was in love with. I gave it to this guy named Bonifide to read and Bonifide said, "No, you can't steal from God." He hit me with the biggest challenge I'd ever faced: "You've got to be honest, Jimmy." When you're a street kid, you can't be honest. Especially if you're in love with a woman; you have to tell her the car is yours, even if you stole it. If you admit to yourself that you have nothing and you are no one, the next step is suicide. I couldn't go there. So, I wrote a poem saying that I had nothing but this poem to give her.

Q: You sent her the poem?

JSB: Yes. Then, believe it or not, someone came to see me. I thought it was my brother, but it was Teresa, the woman I was in love with. She'd come all the way from Chicago. A *poem* made her drive half way across the U.S. to see me.

Q: What was it like to see her after all that time?

JSB: When I saw her, it was devastating because I knew I didn't love her anymore. I had been reading books like *Madame Bovary* and they had changed the DNA structure of how I saw and defined beauty.

It's so sad, a sad thing, when the literature you've been reading redefines your standard of beauty, and the one thing you've been living for is taken from you. I had to make a decision about whether I was going to go out and be a criminal and wreck havoc or pursue literature and find out what was beyond this change.

Q: How did you make that decision?

JSB: When I walked across the yard, I was elated and yet in sorrow. I was experiencing the power of literature. It had actually changed my mind about something. I went back to the cell and wrote a poem to the judge to see if he would release me, but it didn't work. (*Laughter*) By the time I got out I had had my first book of poetry published, *Immigrants in Our Own Land*.

Learning to Read and Write

Q: When you first came to prison, you really couldn't read?

JSB: Well, no, you know, functionally illiterate. Anybody can read *it* or *you* or *a*, *and*, *but*. It's not so much the fact that you can read or not read. I couldn't read, but it's what happens to an individual who is not able to read. What condition does that person fall into?

Q: Did it ever bother you before then that you couldn't read? Were you embarrassed by it?

JSB: Never embarrassed.

Q: So how did you start to read?

JSB: Well, there was a guy named Harry, who was a good Samaritan in Phoenix, who wrote me a letter asking what I needed for Christmas. You know, he picked my name out of a hat and said, "It's Christmastime, you don't have anybody to visit or anybody to visit you, so what would you like?" And, I told him, "Could you send me a book, an English and Spanish book?" And he did.

When I began to read, I began very slowly, and I had these books that had English and Spanish on opposing pages. The material was very rudimentary, elementary, kind of religious teachings. Now what happened was that I would read most of the day and into the night, and I would pronounce the language aloud. I pronounced adjectives and adverbs and nouns and prepositions and so forth aloud, and then early in the morning I would wake up and begin to write in a journal.

Q: What sorts of things were you recording there? Words, thoughts, feelings, memories?

JSB: I was writing things that I remembered doing as a kid and as an adult and so forth. And what happened was that, in a place like prison where you are deprived of all sensory enjoyment, language became more real, more tangible than bars or concrete, than the structure of buildings in the landscape. So I began to read, to read and write in the sense that, metaphorically, I wrapped myself in this cocoon of language, and when I came back out, I was no longer the caterpillar: I was a butterfly.

Q: You used your newfound literacy in prison to help other convicts?

JSB: I started writing letters and poems, and reading for the convicts. They gave me coffee, cigarettes, pencils and tablets, and I started a very thriving ordering system.

Q: Do you remember anything you wrote, any of the letters or poems that you wrote for other people inside?

JSB: I remember the first stanza I ever wrote in my life. I was naked in the shower. I was in prison, and I think I was reading Turgenev. I soaped myself up, and all of a sudden I got hit with a lightning bolt. You know how they call it the "muse"? I call it the "Mohammed Ali left hook." These lines came to me, and I ran out of the shower naked and the guard hit the alarm button, because you can't run, you know?

Besides, there goes a naked Mexican running down the hall, what are you going to do? He hit the alarm button, and I ran into my cell with soapy hands and stuff, and wrote down these six lines of poetry. And then of course, the soap got in my eyes and reality came back and I had to rush back to the shower to wash the soap off. But at that point I think I was classified as a nutcase.

Q: Do you remember the lines?

JSB: The poem was a response to a group of senators who had been touring the prison the previous day, examining the aftermath of a riot. The lines were "Did you tell them, that hell is not a dream, that you've been there, did you tell them?"

Q: Were you able to read it to someone after you wrote it?

JSB: Ah, no . . . except for the birds, the trees, and the air, the dust, and the sun outside my window.

JSB: My goal in life was to be an English teacher. So, what I was writing, I wasn't particularly gung ho about having people hear it, or even read it, because I didn't think I was a poet, I didn't think I was a writer, I was simply trying to grasp the language. And, in doing so, I kept a journal. I kept many journals.

Q: You first began to write poetry in prison, publishing in *Mother Jones*' literary section that was edited at the time by Denise Levertov. Why this magazine?

JSB: *Mother Jones* was doing the Black Panther inquiry, the killing of George Jackson in prison, so it was all over the prison. Some guy threw the magazine in my cell and said, "Hey, they're paying a hundred bucks a poem." I didn't know how to put the stamp or the address on the letter or anything, but I took my shoebox and grabbed a bunch of poems that I had written. And I sent them to a place called San Francisco—never expecting to hear back from them, but they published the poems internationally and sent me 300 bucks, and I was like, wow! I thought I could be rich off of poetry—that was a really naïve assumption!

Q: So, was the $300 held for you until you were released?

JSB: No. I put it in my store. I bought ice cream for all of death row and all of segregation. I just splurged.

Q: You treated everybody?

JSB: Yeah, since everybody had been supporting me for a few years, I decided it was my turn to give them something. That was one cold day in hell.

The Power of Language

Q: You love language, you say. You've called it almost a physical thing for you.

JSB: Oh, I love language. I love language. Language, to me, is what sunrise is to the birds. Language, to me, is what water is to a man that just crossed the desert. I remember, as a boy, grown-ups looked like huge redwood trees to me in a storm, or they looked like boats without a map in a bad storm at sea. And the grown-ups in my life were always caught up in dramas. And the one thing that they all had in common was they couldn't express that storm inside of themselves. And I was so caught up in that drama that I vowed one day I would grasp hold of the power that could evoke their emotions. For me, at least, I wanted to know how to say what was happening to them and I wanted to name things.

Q: How were you able to find the power of language in prison?

JSB: I had been writing poems to the convicts' daughters and wives. One day a stone straight-up killer came to my cell and said "I want you to write a poem to my mom up in Alabama." I said it would cost him a carton of cigarettes. I wrote it and it was my first opportunity to go into that place where my mother had abandoned me at 5 years old. I went back to that period and I remembered playing with my mother's hair. I got so deep into that poem, it shook every tendon in my body. When the killer came back to my cell, he said, "Read it," because he didn't know how to read. As I began to read the poem, I noticed his knuckles turned purple on the bars and his face was turning red. That's not a good sign because he could kill me. I wondered if something happened in the poem where I had insulted his mother. So I handed it to him and said, "Take the poem," and he said, "You read it," and stared at me with a glazed rage. When I finished reading the poem, he said something I will never forget. He said, "How does a Mexi-can know what's in a white man's heart?" I knew right then and there I had a power that was endless.

Q: Did the other convicts sense this power?

JSB: Well, when I would read to the convicts, there was a sense of awe, my awe, their awe, and at the same time a sense of vulnerability, of my, our vul-nerability. In other words, language had such a tremendous power, and then, in many instances with convicts, language was the very tool that had been used to destroy them and their families.

Q: How?

JSB: For example, when their mothers and fathers had gone into offices to ask about taxes and didn't know how to speak English, they were assault-ed with English, by this same language. It was their mothers and fathers who had gone to courts and not understood the English language and were too proud to ask for interpreters. You see, the pride of these people comes from the fact that they had been living on this land for anywhere from 500 to 2,000 years. They had a direct family lineage of living on the land, and of the many catastrophes and tragedies that occurred in their lives, one could trace most directly to their inability to understand the English language.

Q: The ability to access language, then, goes much deeper than simply knowing how to read and write?

JSB: A remarkable thing occurred to me when I came upon language, and I really began to evoke language to de-create me and then to give birth to me again. What I experienced was this: when you approach language in this being-reborn sense, you approach language in the way that the Hopis approach language, which is that language is a very real living being. I approach it as if it will contain who I am as a person. Now, when language begins to work itself on you and make certain demands of you, it begins to ask you to risk yourself and walk along its edge.

Q: Which is what happened with you.

JSB: Which is what happened with me—I gave birth to myself.

Q: Did language have this potential for you all of your life?

JSB: I can distinctly remember when we didn't have anything to eat, as a child, when my grandfather would begin to sing all these songs. And the songs slowly but surely would end up taking our hunger away.

About Writing

Q: So, you developed your own sense of language. I mean, you had it obviously with you, but you began writing and reading in a kind of personal effort.

JSB: I had a blinding reverence for life in its loving form, and I had a blinding terror of life in its violent form. And I found myself literally scattered between those two poles of terror of life and love of life, that language I began to beckon and beg. I began to beg like a dog at the back door of words. I would beg that these words give me sustenance in the same way we feed our body food. Please give me something to live for, and it was that cataclysmic faith, it was the Armageddon of love and faith, and all of that. The idea of fatality, that life will end today, and I must have one truth, and it really literally could have because I had contracts on me to be killed because I refused to quit writing and so forth. Well, I begged that I live, or at least let me say one thing in life, let someone know I was alive, let someone know that Jimmy Santiago Baca came to Earth. Please let me leave something.

Q: What were your models at that time for being a poet?

JSB: What sustained me through the darkest periods, when I thought I might die, when I was having nervous breakdowns, were the Mexican poets and the Spanish poets who unceasingly gave passion to the work, gave passion to the language. They didn't write poetry that said, "Well, I went down to the store. . . ." No, they said, "I MUST go to the STORE!" And it was at these weak moments when I felt myself fragmenting in my entire existence, falling away like sand through my fingers. I couldn't keep it together. It was falling away from me. I would passionately open up Pablo

Neruda, Federico García Lorca, Jaime Sabines, and these voices would say to me, "Fight Santiago, you get up and fight, don't let the darkness take you. *Hijo d'su. Y despues de leer como un poeta como Neruda, me levante, y va uno recio adelante.*" To translate that, I said, after reading Pablo Neruda, I would stand up and give this hardy howl, woof, woof, come, I'm ready.

Q: I can see that in your writing too. Your writing is full of that kind of energy. Let's talk about how you write now that you have made your mark on the world.

JSB: I start writing and I write very eclectically. I'm sort of eccentric in the sense that I'll write ten minutes and get up, walk around, sit down, write five minutes, get up, walk around. I'll do different things according to what I'm writing. With *Healing Earthquakes*, I had a different approach. I sat down and just wrote passionately, a burst, a shower burst so to speak. When I'm writing something else like short stories or a novel, they each have their different approaches that affect me physically and that I follow physically. So that's how I do it.

Q: You enjoy each of those processes equally?

JSB: What we love, we have no control over.

Q: How do you perceive yourself as a writer?

JSB: One of the interesting things about being a writer in America is if you don't come with all the credentials, it's pretty hard to be comfortable calling yourself a writer. I wasn't comfortable until I was in my early 40s when I began to say, "I'm a writer." But, I still hadn't written *A Place to Stand*; it was still looming in the distance, saying, "You ain't nothin' till you deal with this." Since writing *A Place to Stand*, I have become very comfortable with the idea that I'm a writer.

Q: What advice do you give to young people who want to become writers?

JSB: When I teach in colleges or universities, I'm struck by the students' unwillingness to risk. It's debilitating to them, this fear. I tell them, "Don't write the way I write or the way Ezra Pound writes. Do it like a rock, a tree." But they're scared, really scared, and they can't do it.

If you really are a writer, then write. Writers write. They don't sit there thinking, "Oh, I need six more credits for this, and four more credits for that." Bottom line, writers write. They soak up everyday experiences then transform this into something else in the process of writing.

About Poetry

Q: How did you come to poetry?

JSB: I put the gun down and picked up the pen.

Q: How did poetry affect you while in prison?

JSB: I don't know if I would have lived had I not found poetry. The thing about poetry is that early on I came to it in prison in such a way that society was not going to accept me, so I then had to bring society to me through my poetry. I had to write the kind of poetry that was accessible and yet which would not compromise my experience, so that society would say, "Oh we understand what he's writing about, and we think that the poetry's okay." And my life has always been sort of like that, about unendingly learning about all the mistakes I made and never being so stupid as to not try to learn something new from my children or from the earth or from friends.

Q: What inspires you to write poetry?

JSB: What inspires you to breathe? If you want to live, you breathe.

Q: What influences you the most regarding your poetry?

JSB: Just the extraordinary sweetness of people, or the rage, or the hatred. I can't stand the comfort zone. So many people I know, their parents give them their homes, and they get married and have children, or whatever. That's it. They don't ever go beyond that. That's not what life is, you know? People say what distinguishes us from the animals is that we think. Well, then why the hell don't we extend some compassion to those under tremendous duress? What about getting into the whole melee of poverty and racism and violence and murder and drug addiction? Get in there, roll up your sleeves, and do something! I believe it's our responsibility as citizens to get in there and not accept the constant failure of prisons to deal with racism, lack of privilege, and impoverishment—to not accept any of that. Just get in there!

Q: Is that conviction something you keep going back to in your poetry?

JSB: Understanding is the key to everything. If I'm making a sandwich, and I'm peeling an avocado, as a poet I represent myself; and if I pay attention to what I'm doing with the avocado and I write a poem about the avocado, then representing myself is representing the avocado—I am the avocado. Poetry extends in ways that don't limit it. It gives you a brief view of the intense beauty of life.

Q: Poetry for you is in every moment?

JSB: It is in the canyons of the bone. I don't try to harvest my poetry from what happens in society's institutions as much as I try to reap the poems from what's happening behind the boundaries of society.

Q: You've said that when you were a young man in prison that discovering language and learning how to write saved you, that you were reborn through poetry.

JSB: For some people, prison actually helps them; they're told what to do, how to dress, and they accept that. Some people shouldn't be let out—they would create havoc in society. But when I was in prison, I realized that I had gotten caught up, that I didn't belong there. The only avenue of escape open to me was to plunge myself into language, into reading. When I did that, it was as if all the walls around me crumbled down, all the wire fences. When I found poetry, it was like being sucked into a shooting star. The epicenter of that attraction was that it taught me how to love myself. I saw how a poem could embrace a paltry, scared human being like me.

Q: Do you remember a specific poem that started this process?

JSB: Actually it was a story by the Russian writer Turgenev about a man going out in the morning and hunting that I connected with. Then there was Emily Dickinson, Ezra Pound. Dickinson had a self-imposed exile and isolation that I understood.

Q: Those writers helped you find yourself as a poet?

JSB: I always felt that there was this body that Jimmy Santiago Baca inhabited in the here and now but that there was also an ephemeral aspect of myself, floating beyond myself. Reading poetry connected with this. It was as if I had been wearing a mask, and poetry allowed me to put on my real face.

Q: The widespread response to your work, from Los Angeles to Boston, suggests that many Americans are in need of the healing power of language. Do you think that is true?

JSB: Corporate power has laid itself on our shoulders, thrown us into the rapids, carried us along so that we live in a state of constant desperation and confusion. We're fragmented, to a point of no return. We need spiritual balance. We need a way to hold onto one another. Poetry can provide that.

Teaching Life

Q: You know what a difference being able to read made for you. Is that why you work with the kids, the gangbangers, steelworkers, convicts, and illiterate adults?

JSB: Damn right. Right into the barrios and the projects and the poor white areas. They have such a reverence for language. They can't believe the language can carry so much power, and once they get hold of that, they begin to unteach what they were taught about who they are.

If they were taught to be racist or violent, language has this amazing ability to unteach all that, and make them question it. It gives them back their power toward regaining their humanity. That's why I do it. Not out of any academic or scholarly incentive.

Q: Where do you begin to "unteach"?

JSB: The whole thing is this: If you don't use just basic grammar, if you don't get the language down, you're not going to have access to a tool that people use as a weapon against you. The only reason I was never taught to read and write was because it was easier for them to lead me. But the second I learned to read and write, I began to lead myself.

Q: You believe everyone has a chance at life through language. . . .

JSB: Prisoners might be illiterate, but, boy, are they intelligent. Education is the key. There are proven educational models right now that are stopping recidivism, racism, and violence in prisons.

Q: How did you begin to become a teacher?

JSB: When I came out of prison, I was given the Wallace Stevens chair at Yale and I went there and also worked in New York. One Christmas I went back to Albuquerque and I gave out books; that's all I had to give. Every person I gave a book to would say, "What's this word? What's that word?" Then, a gentleman came up to me and said something that was really remarkable, that was sort of a reckoning, a pivotal reckoning. "Instead of being at Yale, why don't you come here where we need you? Because I don't know how to read." I went back to New Haven and told them I couldn't stay any longer.

I started my first writing workshop in Albuquerque at St. Anne's church, in a barrack behind the church; thirty years ago we had our first poetry workshop. Since then, I've gone back into prisons. We are working in a women's prison now, in McLoud, Oklahoma, with forty-one women who have committed murder. We are doing a documentary there.

Q: You have established a nonprofit for your work?

JSB: Cedar Tree, Inc., is my nonprofit and we do so much. Through the grace of God we get donations in the mail and we continue the work. We do workshops with homeless teens, inmates at Soledad State Prison, and kids in a juvenile detention center. We did a project at an unwed mothers' school called "Don't Hit Me" and then we did a project at the juvenile center where we tried to teach kids not to hit. We did it all through literature.

Q: You have said that your work with kids keeps your own voice strong.

JSB: I don't dismiss the academic and scholarly sectors of society. I go listen to what they say, and I read what they write. But it's not near as exciting as hearing language invented from experiences that have truly been lived, almost, in many cases, on the verge of dying. I've never heard a professor stand up and say, "I'll give my life for this," and yet I listen to these kids and they say, "I'll give up my life, I put my life on the line with this poem about my mom." And I'm like, "Wow." That keeps educating me about where my poetry should be.

Q: Is it hard to "break into" the lives of people with whom you work?

JSB: We put ourselves in places where we serve. When I work with at-risk kids who haven't had much education and I tell them I'm going to read them some words, and I see some smiles or a look of recognition as they respond to these words, this nurtures me. After a period of weeks, a trust, a familial attachment develops. We're one, we care for each other.

Q: You help kids become a part of a community.

JSB: We all want to be included. If I can go into a classroom and include this young girl, she also includes me in her life. I feel so empowered that when I leave, I feel I could open a door just by thinking about opening a door!

Q: How does literacy, teaching kids to speak, write, and appreciate literature, support this process?

JSB: There are all these divisions in our lives. When I go into the neighborhood, I see kids who despise anyone successful or anyone different than they are. I tell them, "This isn't being a man, spreading hatred of people who are not like you." But the clarion call of our day seems to be opposition, you must oppose something. Poetry melts these differences. Reading does it. I die every time I read a book. It's so wonderful to forget that I exist. I want to thank the writer for letting me in. I'm grateful that there are writers out there who can give me this. It's there, this salvation and redemption. All we have to do is pick up a novel or a poem to find this.

Q: You once wrote that in your teens you had become the coauthor with society of your own oppression. What are you coauthoring with society now?

JSB: I want to coauthor the lessening of rage in prisons and the racism and the addiction that's killing so many young kids. I've dealt with my racism. I used to hate blacks and whites. I used to hate my own kind. I've dealt with that. And with my violence, with drug addiction, where I used to be an addict because I couldn't deal with the pain. I have dealt with that in the most nightmarish loneliness and have come out the other end of that, healthy and whole.

How to Use the DVD with Your Students and Colleagues

The DVD included in this book can be used for a variety of purposes, both in the classroom with your students and in professional development settings.

The following guide is organized to mirror the structure of the DVD menu. Following the name of each DVD segment, you will find:

- Activities to engage students for each story Jimmy tells on the DVD

- "Classroom Practice," which provides suggestions for using class-room footage of students working with Jimmy and ReLeah to enhance and extend your own students' learning

- "Professional Development" sections designed to expand your under-standing of the material, by yourself or with colleagues.

Jimmy's Story

The companion story to this video segment, "The Journey to Be Loved" (page 79), may be a difficult read for some students, especially if they have little background knowledge about Jimmy's life or work. Before students begin reading "The Journey to Be Loved," allow them to view "Jimmy's

Story" on the DVD. After viewing, ask students to respond to the story in writing. They may use the following prompts to guide their responses.

- Do any of the students on the video remind you of friends or classmates?

- Jimmy discusses how he didn't have a family, a house, a future. "I wanted respect, love, companionship," he said. What would you say that you want most in life?

- Respond to Jimmy's statements about education and reading: "I get my education or I die" and "I would have died had I not been able to open a book." How are these statements similar to or different from the way you feel about reading or gaining an education?

Saving the Tree

The written account of "Saving the Tree" (page 138) is much shorter than the version Jimmy tells on the DVD. Just as we watch movies and then want to see the "extras," students will have the opportunity to find out more about this story as Jimmy elaborates. After they view this segment, have students talk in small groups about how oral storytelling differs from a written account. Discuss how intonation, gestures, and interaction with the listeners enhance the story. Allow groups to share their observations.

Show students this segment again, asking them to keep notes about specific details that Jimmy provides that are not in the text. Then, still in groups, have students create a storyboard on chart paper, incorporating details from both accounts. Go to http://accad.osu.edu/womenandtech/Storyboard%20Resource/ for more information about creating storyboards.

Engaging Students in Dialogue and Reflection

Classroom Practice

Use this segment to show your students how peers in a community talk with one another. Encourage them to participate in the dialogue by raising their hands when they have something to add to the discussion taking place on the screen, perhaps something they may want to say to one of the teens on the DVD—or to offer an answer to a question ReLeah poses.

Professional Development

While watching this segment alone or with other teachers, note ways your students are different from or similar to the students in the video. Chart how ReLeah's methods can be used with your own students or how you may need to alter her methods to meet your students' individualized needs.

Freewriting with Students

Classroom Practice

You may choose to allow ReLeah to guide your students in this freewriting exercise, if for no other reason than to give students a different "teacher" for the activity. In this segment, Jimmy makes a point that extends the theme of the story, so you will want to allow your students to view this part of the video. As students in the DVD share their writing, Jimmy begins talking about loss. "Don't be afraid to express your loss," he says. Depending on your class, you may use this as a jumping-off point for students to write about their own losses.

Professional Development

This segment focuses on freewriting. ReLeah tells students that the writing they are doing is not for a grade; that, in fact, it "belongs" to the writer. Discuss this philosophy with other teachers, addressing the point that students may be reluctant to participate if their writing is "not for a grade." How can this attitude be changed so that students come to "own" writing rather than seeing it as just one more burdensome assignment?

Additionally, you may wish to discuss how this activity serves to develop community within this particular group of students, especially since they did not know one another well before working together on this video. Note, too, that certain types of personal writing, such as writing about poignant topics, increases community as students come to know each other by sharing common experiences.

Writing Prompt

Classroom Practice

ReLeah provides a prompt that will resonate with all students. "If there is one thing that you would want people to know to better understand you, what would it be?" Allow your students to respond to this same prompt, writing and sharing with a partner first and then in small groups, as a way of building trust. ReLeah refers to a young adult novel titled *You Don't Know Me* by David Klass, which your students may enjoy reading.

Professional Development

As you watch this segment, note that ReLeah asks students what they need to do before writing, thus turning the responsibility back to them about how they will begin. She also asks if they need more time instead of giving them a specified amount of time in which to write. Discuss with other teachers the extent to which students in your school have choices over their writing—before, during, and after the process.

Students Share Their Writing

Classroom Practice

Place students in small groups or with partners. After each student on the video speaks, stop the DVD and have your students respond to what was said. Encourage your class to use the speaker's points as a springboard for discussion, but be clear in your expectations: your students are as capable of engaging in a meaningful discussion as those on the DVD. You may then want to facilitate a whole-class discussion, especially after Jimmy makes his point about the roots of trees sending out signals. Ask your class how that metaphor works within their class, school, or community.

Professional Development

ReLeah models an important aspect of community dialogue, having students talk with each other rather than the traditional teacher-to-student talk. Have another teacher come into your classroom and observe a class discussion. Specifically, your peer should note how often students direct comments to you and how often they speak with one another, noting as well what comments you make that encourage interclass dialogue.

Man on the Beach

Jimmy begins this story by saying, "Let me tell you a story about *stereotypes*." Pause the DVD here and explore students' understanding of this word. This is a term that may have different meanings based on each individual's life experiences. Have students work with a partner to discover the shades of meaning behind this complex word by creating a graphic organizer. For example, students could fold a piece of paper into fourths and in each quadrant answer questions, such as the following, regarding the word *stereotype*.

- What does it mean to stereotype someone?
- What is the opposite of stereotyping?
- Draw a cartoon that defines stereotyping.
- How can stereotypes be eliminated in your world?

Writing Prompt and Student Discussion

Classroom Practice

Just as ReLeah asks students on the DVD what this story triggered from their own experiences, your students will also remember times when they have been stereotyped or have stereotyped others. If you decide to show this segment to students, do it *after* they have had a chance to engage in a dialogue with their own peers about their experiences with stereotypes.

Professional Development

Students who learn to think with question marks in their minds are actively involved in the learning process. Often, teachers fall into the habit of asking questions and then waiting for students to answer. After you watch this segment with your peers, discuss how you can move students from "question answerers" to "question askers." For example, students may jot down questions they have as others talk, write questions on sticky-notes as they read, or work with a partner to come up with questions they would like to ask Jimmy about his stories.

ReLeah mentioned *The Education of Little Tree* by Forrest Carter, a book that would further the discussions generated in this video.

Role-Playing

Classroom Practice

Having students assume another person's perspective is a valuable practice, as it moves writers from their own viewpoints to a broader understanding of others. The activity for this story could be altered by having students write from other vantage points: Jimmy's, Jimmy's wife, Jimmy's child, or even the dog's.

Professional Development

As you watch this segment, notice how often the students laugh as they engage in role-playing. Having fun while immersed in literacy sends a message to students that reading, writing, speaking, and performing can be as enjoyable as out-of-school activities. Look through Chapter 6, "Performances and Projects," to help you plan a pleasurable literacy experience with your students.

Tractor-Trailer Moments

Without introduction, show students this segment, allowing them to hear the story for the first time just as the teens in the video hear the story. Tell students that when Jimmy gives the writing prompt, they, too, should write. Make sure that the room is quiet as students process the story in their own way and then begin writing. This may be one of those pieces that is too private for students to share. They may wish to save the writing in their portfolios, give it to someone they trust to read, or dispose of it in any way they choose. Such an approach conveys to students that writing has many different purposes, one of which is that it can be a powerful vehicle for better understanding themselves.

Writing Prompt and Student Discussion

Classroom Practice

If your students write about the prompt that was given in the earlier segment, you may want to try the activity Jimmy demonstrates with these students. He encourages them to share without having them read their entire piece to others in the class. They can summarize the main points in their papers or simply talk about one part—it's their choice. Giving students choice in deciding what they will share with others allows them to gain autonomy over their writing, leading to an increased sense of self-efficacy.

Professional Development

As you watch this video with peers, you will note that that the students are a model of respect—both toward their classmates and toward the teacher. Discuss with others in your school ways that you can develop such a culture of respect. While the process may take time, you can use this video with students as well as with the entire faculty to help them define the characteristics of mutual respect.

American Dream

Before having students view this segment, lead them in a discussion of what the "American dream" means to them. Write the term on the board with the following questions to prompt discussion in small groups or with partners:

- What does "American dream" mean to *you*?
- In what way is the "American dream" different for various segments of America?
- How do you plan to achieve your own American dream?
- What was the American dream for your parents? Their parents?

End-of-Unit Reflection

Classroom Practice

The practice of asking students to reflect on what they have learned can take several forms. Students may respond orally, as they did on the DVD, or you can provide activities, such as exit cards or end-of-unit surveys, that require students to answer questions similar to the following:

- What was most difficult for you to do (or learn) in this lesson?
- What one thing that another student said helped with your understanding?
- What is something that I, as your teacher, could have done to help you with this lesson?
- What was the most valuable part of this activity for you?

Professional Development

Asking students to reflect on what they have learned, either regarding a specific lesson or a unit of study, increases students' metacognition. As you watch this segment with peers, discuss how you can use students' comments about what they learned to help you become a better teacher. In various content areas, this activity may look different, but devoting time to this practice in your classroom will help you come to know your students better and give them the opportunity to significantly contribute to their own learning.

Jimmy and ReLeah talk with teachers about "adolescents on the edge"

This section of the DVD is divided into topics pertinent to the themes of this book and can be used in a variety of ways.

- Individually, teachers can view segments that are of interest to them, perhaps responding in writing as a way of deepening or reinforcing their own understandings.
- Within teams or departments, teachers can view one segment at a time, using each as a springboard for discussion and subsequent action. For example, in the segment on assessing writing, ReLeah expresses views with which teachers may or may not agree. In any case, many districts, schools, and teachers grapple with assessment. Use this segment as the introduction to a study group on ways to assess writing.

- Literacy coaches often must provide schoolwide professional development for the rest of the faculty. The segments on this part of the video highlight subjects that could be the basis for longer study sessions. Or, the faculty as a whole might view one of the segments at a monthly faculty meeting and discuss the content in small groups as a way of encouraging dialogue about curricular topics.
- The first six chapters of *Adolescents on the Edge* offer titles of books for additional study based on the topic of the chapter. Using that list and the related pieces in this segment, curriculum developers on the school or district level could create professional development offerings for a summer workshop, inservice days, or ongoing, embedded staff development in the form of book and video studies.

References

Alvermann, Donna, E. 2003. *Seeing Themselves as Capable and Engaged Readers: Adolescents and Remediated Instruction*. Naperville, IL: Learning Point Associates.

Ancess, Jacqueline. 2008. "Small Alone Is Not Enough." *Educational Leadership* 54 (May): 48–53.

Azzam, Amy, M. 2008. "Engaged and on Track." *Educational Leadership* 65 (March): 93–94.

Baca, Jimmy S. 1990. "The Handsome World," "Jewelry Store," and "I Am with Those." In *Immigrants in Our Own Land & Selected Early Poems*. New York: New Directions.

———. 2001. *A Place to Stand*. New York: Grove Press.

———. 2007. "Ancestors Run Next to Me" and "Spring Arrives." In *Spring Poems Along the Rio Grande*. New York: New Directions.

———. 2009. Email correspondence to ReLeah Cossett Lent.

———. n.d. Unpublished draft of story, "Only His Voice," sent to ReLeah Cossett Lent in July 2009.

Block, Peter. 2008. *Community: The Structure of Belonging*. San Francisco: Berrett-Koehler.

Cambourne, Brian. 1988. *The Whole Story: Natural Learning and the Acquisition of Literacy in the Classroom*. New York: Scholastic.

———. 1995. "Toward an Educationally Relevant Theory of Literacy Learning: Twenty Years of Inquiry." *The Reading Teacher* 49 (November): 182–90.

Carter, Forrest. 2001. *The Education of Little Tree*. Albuquerque: University of New Mexico Press.

Daniels, Harvey, and Nancy Steineke. 2004. *Mini-Lessons for Literature Circles*. Portsmouth, NH: Heinemann.

Darling-Hammond, Linda, and Diane Friedlander. 2008. "Creating Excellent *and* Equitable Schools." *Educational Leadership* 65: 14–21.

Debold, Elizabeth. 2002. "Flow with Soul: An Interview with Dr. Mihaly Csikszentmihalyi." *Enlightenment Magazine* (Spring/Summer). Available at www.enlightennext.org/magazine/j21/csiksz.asp?page=2.

Dillard, Annie. 1990. *The Writing Life*. New York: HarperCollins.

Editorial Projects in Education. 2008. "Diplomas Count. School to College: Can State P–16 Councils Ease the Transition?" *Education Week* 27 (40). Available at www.edweek.org/ew/toc/2008/06/05/index.html

Gallagher, Chris, and Amy Lee. 2008. *Teaching Writing That Matters: Tools and Projects That Motivate Adolescent Writers*. New York: Scholastic.

Gallagher, Kelly. 2006. *Teaching Adolescent Writers*. Portland, ME: Stenhouse.

Gilmore, Barry. 2006. *Speaking Volumes: How to Get Students Discussing Books—and Much More*. Portsmouth, NH: Heinemann.

———. 2007. *Is It Done Yet? Teaching Adolescents the Art of Revision*. Portsmouth, NH: Heinemann.

Goddard, Yvette L., Roger D. Goddard, and Megan Tschannen-Moran. 2007. "A Theoretical and Empirical Investigation of Teacher Collaboration for School Improvement and Student Achievement in Public Elementary Schools." *Teacher College Record*. Available (with login) at www.tcrecord.org/PrintContent.asp?ContentID=12871.

Goswami, Usha. 2008. "Neuroscience and Education." In *The Jossey-Bass Reader on the Brain and Learning*, 33–50. San Francisco: Jossey-Bass.

Gruwell, Erin, Z. Filipovic, and Freedom Writers. 1999. *The Freedom Writers Diary*. New York: Broadway Books.

Heathcote, Dorothy. 1995. *Drama for Learning: Dorothy Heathcote's Mantle of the Expert Approach to Education*. Portsmouth, NH: Heinemann.

Hillocks, George Jr. 1986. *Research on Written Composition: New Directions for Teaching*. Urbana, IL: Educational Resources Information Center and NCTE.

Jensen, Eric. 2006. *Enriching the Brain: How to Maximize Every Learner's Potential*. San Francisco: Jossey-Bass.

Kamil, Michael L. 2003. *Adolescents and Literacy: Reading for the 21st Century*. Washington, DC: Alliance for Excellent Education.

Khadaroo, Stacy T. 2009. "Schools Tap '21st-Century Skills.'" *Christian Science Monitor*, 8 January. Available at www.csmonitor.com/2009/0108/p03s03-usgn.html.

Klass, David. 2001. *You Don't Know Me*. New York: Farrar, Straus & Giroux.

Kuni, Page. 2009. "Learning Environments Must Break Through the Silos That Separate Learning from the Real World." 23 January. Available at www.21stcenturyskills.org/index.php?option=com_content&task=view&id=598&Itemid=64http://www.21stcenturyskills.org/index.php?option=com_content&task=view&id=598&Itemid=64.

Lent, ReLeah. 2006. *Engaging Adolescent Learners: A Guide for Content-Area Teachers*. Portsmouth, NH: Heinemann.

———. 2007. *Literacy Learning Communities: A Guide for Creating Sustainable Change in Secondary Schools*. Portsmouth: NH: Heinemann.

———. 2009. *Literacy for Real: Reading, Thinking, and Learning in the Content Areas*. New York: Teachers College Press.

Meier, Deborah. 1995. *The Power of Their Ideas: Lessons from a Small School in Harlem*. Boston: Beacon.

Nair, Prakash. 2009. "Don't Just Rebuild Schools—Reinvent Them." *Education Week*, April 6. Available (with login) at www.edweek.org/ew/articles/2009/04/0828nair_ep.h28.html?tkn=ZPLFK9zdEjQoc.

National Commission on Writing in America's Schools and Colleges. 2003. *The Neglected "R": The Need for a Writing Revolution*. New York: College Entrance Examination Board.

National Council of Teachers of English, Commission on Composition. 1985. "Teaching Composition: A Position Statement." Available at www.ncte.org/positions/statements/teachingcomposition.

National Research Council. 2000. *How People Learn: Brain, Mind, Experience, and School*. Washington, DC: National Academy Press.

National Writing Project, and Carl Nagin. 2006. *Because Writing Matters: Improving Student Writing in Our Schools*. San Francisco: Jossey-Bass.

Newkirk, Thomas, and Richard Kent, eds. 2007. *Teaching the Neglected "R": Rethinking Writing Instruction in Secondary Classrooms*. Portsmouth, NH: Heinemann.

Nieto, Sonia. 1999. *The Light in Their Eyes: Creating Multicultural Learning Communities*. New York: Teachers College Press.

Noddings, Nel. 2005. *The Challenge to Care in Schools: An Alternative Approach to Education*, 2d ed. New York: Teachers College Press.

North Central Regional Educational Laboratory. 2005. *Implementing No Child Left Behind: Using Student Engagement to Improve Adolescent Literacy.* Available at www.ncrel.org/policy/curve/resource.htm#resources.

Palmer, Parker. 1998. *The Courage to Teach*. San Francisco: Jossey-Bass.

Quate, Stevi, and John McDermott. 2009. *Clock Watchers: Six Steps to Motivating and Engaging Disengaged Students Across Content Areas.* Portsmouth, NH: Heinemann.

Restak, Richard. 2008. "How Our Brain Constructs Our Mental World." In *Jossey-Bass Reader on the Brain and Learning*. San Franciso: Jossey-Bass.

Rosenblatt, Louise. 2005. *Making Meaning with Texts: Selected Essays.* Portsmouth, NH: Heinemann.

Roskelly, Hephzibah. 2003. *Breaking (into) the Circle: Group Work for Change in the English Classroom*. Portsmouth, NH: Boynton/Cook.

Smith, Michael W., and Jeffrey D. Wilhelm. 2002. *"Reading Don't Fix No Chevys": Literacy in the Lives of Young Men*. Portsmouth, NH: Heinemann.

———. 2006. *Going with the Flow: How to Engage Boys (and Girls) in Their Literacy Learning*. Portsmouth, NH: Heinemann.

Stracener, Dawn. 2009. Personal communication via email message to ReLeah Cossett Lent, August 18.

Strickland, Dorothy S., and Donna E. Alvermann, eds. 2004. *Bridging the Literacy Achievement Gap Grades 4–12*. New York: Teachers College Press.

Surowiecki, James. 2004. *The Wisdom of Crowds*. New York: Anchor.

Sylwester, Robert. 2008. "Alphabetized Entries from How to Explain a Brain." In *Jossey-Bass Reader on the Brain and Learning*. San Francisco: Jossey-Bass.

Tatum, Alfred. 2009. *Reading for Their Life: Building Textual Lineages for African American Males*. Portsmouth, NH: Heinemann.

Tomlinson, Carol A. 2003. *Fulfilling the Promise of the Differentiated Classroom: Strategies and Tools for Responsive Teaching*. Alexandria, VA: Association for Supervision and Curriculum Development.

Torgesen, Joseph K., Debra D. Houston, Lila M. Rissman, Susan M. Decker, Greg Roberts, Sharon Vaughn, David Francis, Mabel O. Rivera, and Nonie Lesaux. 2007. *Academic Literacy Instruction for*

Adolescents: A Guidance Document from the Center on Instruction. Portsmouth, NH: RMC Research Corporation, Center on Instruction.

Tschannen-Moran, Megan. 2004. *Trust Matters: Leadership for Successful Schools.* San Francisco: Jossey-Bass.

VanderHeyden, Andrea. 2008. "What Students Want from Teachers." *Educational Leadership* 66: 50.

Vygotsky, Lev. 1978. *Mind in Society: Development of Higher Psychological Processes.* Cambridge, MA: Harvard University Press.

Washington, Booker T. 1963. *Up from Slavery.* New York: Bantam Books.

Wigfield, Allan. 2004. "Motivation for Reading During the Early Adolescent Years." In *Bridging the Literacy Achievement Gap Grades 4–12,* ed. Dorothy S. Strickland and Donna E. Alvermann, 56–69. New York: Teachers College Press.

Wiggins, Grant, and Jay McTighe. 1998. *Understanding by Design.* Alexandria, VA: Association for Supervision and Curriculum Development.

Wilhelm, Jeffrey D. 2007. *Engaging Readers & Writers with Inquiry: Promoting Deep Understandings in Language Arts and the Content Areas with Guiding Questions.* New York: Scholastic.

———. 2008. *"You Gotta BE the Book": Teaching Engaged and Reflective Reading with Adolescents.* New York: Teachers College Press.

Winter, Jonah. 2002. *Frida.* New York: Arthur A. Levine Books.

Wise, Bob. 2009. "Adolescent Literacy: The Cornerstone of Student Success." *Journal of Adolescent & Adult Literacy* 52: 369–75.

Yazzie-Mintz, Ethan. 2006. "Voices of Students on Engagement: A Report on the 2006 High School Survey of Student Engagement." Bloomington, IN: Center for Evaluation & Education Policy.

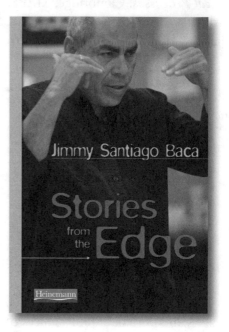